THE CHURCH AND THE
NEW WORLD MIND

THE CHURCH AND THE NEW WORLD MIND

The Drake Lectures for 1944

By

WILLIAM E. HOCKING

WILLMOTT LEWIS

GEORGIA HARKNESS

M. SEARLE BATES

G. BAEZ-CAMARGO

CLEO W. BLACKBURN

WALTER W. VAN KIRK

RUFUS M. JONES

Essay Index Reprint Series
97259

BOOKS FOR LIBRARIES PRESS
FREEPORT, NEW YORK

LIBRARY OF CONGRESS CATALOG CARD NUMBER:
68-57311

PRINTED IN THE UNITED STATES OF AMERICA

FOREWORD

THE Drake Conference on "The Church and the New World Mind" was sponsored by Drake University, and the following organizations of the Disciples of Christ: the United Christian Missionary Society, the Board of Higher Education, and the Association for the Promotion of Christian Unity. The university served as host.

The lecturers were selected from a wide diversity of personnel, experience, and religious affiliation. While the Disciples of Christ planned the conference, only two of the eight lecturers were drawn from that body. Geographically, they represent the United States of America, Latin America, Great Britain, and the Orient, while the voice of the Negro is blended with that of the Caucasian.

Each of the lecture subjects was studied by one of nine seminar groups assembled in as many important centers. These findings, which represent the realism of laboratory research, became part of the conference discussions and, with these, will be abridged and printed in pamphlet form under the title *The Church and the World Mind—A Study Guide,* to be used in local churches. The members of the Central Committee having charge of the arrangements for the Drake Conference were Hampton Adams, M. Searle Bates, George W. Buckner, Jr., James A. Crain, John L. Davis, Henry G. Harmon, Robert M. Hopkins, C. E.

5

Lemmon, Harold L. Lunger, Raphael H. Miller, Roger
T. Nooe, Wm. F. Rothenburger.

The lectures had very little to say about the war.
This is, in itself, a paradox. For the Drake Conference met at a time of strenuous military effort and
during a period of great battles. This does not mean
that the delegates were disinterested in the war. The
grim necessity for a military victory underscored the
lectures. The absence of discussion of the war does
not mean that the conference was conducted in a
vacuum. Far from it. It means that to churchmen,
the war is but an incident—howbeit, a tragic and terrible incident—in the social revolution of our time.
Churchmen are thinking of the war in the larger context of world life. It is this larger context that
occupies their minds. If it is the duty of the military
leader to think of the next battle, or the next campaign,
it is the duty of the churchman to think in terms of
the generation and its destiny.

The first conference of churchmen held during the
war was at Malvern, England, in January, 1941. It
was a tragic period in British life. London, Plymouth,
and Coventry had been bombed. The outcome of the
war was in grave doubt. The preoccupation of the
British mind with the war was most natural. And
yet, in the midst of this crisis, the Anglican leaders
came to Malvern and issued a manifesto, not on the
war, but on the social wrongs out of which the war
had come and the social changes which were necessary

if the world is to have a durable peace. The church-men at Malvern called the war "one symptom of a widespread disease and maladjustment resulting from loss of conviction concerning the reality and character of God, and the true nature and destiny of man," and proceeded to detail practical recommendations for the life of the church and the order of society.

This assumption of the Malvern Conference that the war is but a deeper symptom of the implicit evils and sins of modern life underlies all the wartime confer-ences of the church. It was the basic assumption of the Delaware conferences of 1942 and 1943. It is the assumption which underlies the Drake Conference in 1944. It is an assumption that is fixing itself in the minds of the people of the Western World. Statesmen are realizing, as they have never done before in war-time, that the winning of the war is not an end in it-self. It is important to win the peace. The winning of the peace will require a hundred times more under-standing, patience, knowledge, and character than the winning of the war. This larger context of the tragic present is the rightful preoccupation of the church, and the lectures of this series indicate that the church is anxious to meet the larger obligation.

The reading of these lectures will indicate the spirit with which the church should approach the problems of the world order. There is in these lectures a sense of moral optimism based on a realistic and compre-hensive view of the problems. Dr. Reinhold Niebuhr has said that Christians always face the danger of being "otherworldly or utopian." There is little danger that the group who heard these lectures or the wider public which reads them will be either. The addresses surely are not otherworldly. On the other hand, they are not utopian. There is an endeavor to face the problems. The careful discussions produce a mood of moral optimism which encourages thought and promotes effort. This mood of informed and realistic optimism, which especially characterizes the lectures of Professor Hocking, is essential if the church is to attain any measure of success in helping produce a new world order.

In fact, Dr. Hocking, by his method of carefully considering and examining all sides of every issue, realistically approaching every problem, and all in a constructive and philosophic spirit, indicates the method and message of religion. The church cannot influence public opinion if it is poorly informed and naïve in its convictions. We cannot exert pressure on the issues if we are loaded with doubts. We cannot be useful if we lack conviction and question our own capacity. Out of conferences like these the true method of constructive effort and useful work is discovered and applied.

Another wholesome and important accent of present-day thought in the church is the realization that the problems of a world order stem from the home life of our own nation. There can be no world order until every nation comes to feel that "peace begins at home." There is not a single world problem but that is illustrated in our own national life. An objective consideration of these problems is essential if our nation is to have a worthy leadership toward the goal of a peaceful world. There has been a careful examination of our own shortcomings in these lectures. Dr. Blackburn has pointed out that the economic inequalities in America illustrate the inequalities in world life; Dr. Bates has shown that our laws with regard to Orientals prejudice a settlement of the Asiatic problem; and Dr. Harkness has indicated that the question of race and racialism cannot be solved on a world basis unless we relieve some of its tensions in our American life. In fact, the grass roots of every world problem can be found in every community. This emphasis on the home base in world affairs has led to some criticism of the lectureship on the ground that we have "failed to speak up for America." The answer to this criticism is that the truest Americanism is to prepare the American mind to work on a basis of equality and justice for the kind of world in which our historic liberties are most congenial.

It is natural for churchmen to sound the note of urgency. It would be idle to pretend to an objective and unbiased discussion of issues. All the discussions are loaded on the side of the persuasiveness of the Christian gospel and the urgency of the world issue. We hear the words of Jesus: "Blessed are the peace-

9

makers.'' We can take no *laissez faire* attitude toward our present crisis. The echoes of this evangelical note are especially evident in the exhortations of Dr. Van Kirk. The church is pressed to action and action now. These are plastic days, and attitudes now formed will determine the weal or woe of mankind for many generations. The day of salvation is at hand.

C. E. LEMMON
Chairman, Central Committee
WM. F. ROTHENBURGER
Executive Director

CONTENTS

11

CONTENTS

FAITH AND WORLD ORDER

William Ernest Hocking

THE general temper of our nation, as I read it to-day, seems to be that of high hope on the military front and low hope on the diplomatic front and on the home front. Many of our people are bracing themselves for disappointment in regard to the shape which the peace will or can take. Many of these people are in the church: they are sober-minded and honest. They do not want to deceive themselves or others. They have seen one fundamental fact of the situation in this or any other war: namely, that war does not *build* civilization; it tears down by its operations and it ruins by its cost. After a great war, all combatants will not merely long for a rest; they will be compelled to do patchwork with available resources. They will have to use whatever grooves of order men have been accustomed to. Radical improvement lies far ahead. The great powers, realizing this situation, have combined their forces to meet it; this is the most auspicious thing that has happened, a truly momentous event. But the question before those powers will not be, What can we build? but, What can we save?

Under these circumstances, many church people feel that the word "faith" itself is a bit untimely; it savors of a will to believe too much, that is, it savors of a certain irresponsibility. What we want in the church, as elsewhere, is a mature "realism."

13

I believe that this temper is important and conscientious—and also helpful. But I come today to bring the church a message first of encouragement and second of duty. This is not the moment either to relax our efforts or to lower our standards.

The church is not likely to get all it aims at; but then the church has never been under the illusion that it would. Good sportsmanship does not promise itself uncontested victory all along the line; but good sportsmanship, no matter what setbacks may occur, never does two things: it never disavows its objective; and it never quits fighting for it until the last whistle. And for whatever it has failed to achieve this time, it is ready to continue the struggle at a later time.

I would not, however, put the matter on the ground of sportsmanship primarily, but on the ground of *reasonable expectation.* I wish to mention swiftly and briefly three grounds for this reasonable expectation, and then go on to enlarge upon one of them.

First is the actual fact of an *increased respect* in which the judgment of the church is held today by many men of affairs. During the last war, it seemed to me that the church suffered a decline in prestige. Not only in Europe and America, but also in Asia, the outbreak of war on such a scale was widely regarded as a failure of the Christian spirit to exert an appreciable influence. The church tended to accept this judgment and to examine itself with humility. We have no reason to feel otherwise today. But we have a wider perspective of the causes of war; and so have the statesmen. Both sides realize that in spite of

14

the defects of the actual church, *it has something* which men and nations need and which they do not know how to find anywhere else.

Further, under this same point, the church now has among its members a greater number of men with a respectable brand of "realism" in their make-ups. This respectable brand consists chiefly in sophistication and common sense: the respectable realist knows the ways of the wicked world without being seduced by them; and he also has good judgment about what can be attempted in the way of improvement; he does not try for an all-round millennium tomorrow. I could mention to you perhaps a dozen respectable realists in the forefront of present-day Protestantism (the Catholic church has for many years been rich in this kind), men who not only can get an audience with members of our State Department, on account of their knowledge and sagacity, but whose advice has frequently been of use to that department. I shall not mention these men by name because, after all, they are many. The church itself has become permeated by this spirit; it knows how to bring "realism" (as a condiment, not as a food) into its spiritual outlook without surrendering its idealism. In this sense, everybody wants to be a realist (and if he wants to be, there is nothing to prevent him, provided he has the necessary union of astuteness and saintliness).

The second ground for expectation is the *plasticity of the future* in our hands at this moment. War does not build, but there is nothing it leaves alone. There is not a social habit it does not disturb, and not a prejudice it does not turn to the sunlight for examination. It is impossible that the postwar world should start where the prewar world left off; it will be either better or worse. The only thing that can prevent its being better is a lack of ideas. The promptitude with which the British church began to examine the foundations of its social order shows the rational way to make use of this situation. What is called for is an intensification of the effort to see clearly where we want the world of tomorrow to go. Men are ready for a crusade if the convincing objective can be defined; they are very much disappointed not to have one.

The third ground for good hope is the *clear analysis* of the world situation which so many have agreed upon that it begins to be an item in public opinion.

It appears first in negative form, namely, that nationalism is a good quality which habitually runs to an impossible excess. In President Wilson's Fourteen Points, the ideal of self-determination of nations was set up in clear language; Point Three of the Atlantic Charter, which announces a "respect" for the right of peoples to choose the form of government under which they shall live, is a more cautious expression of the same ideal. It is an indispensable phase of liberty. But it runs to excess in two ways: first, by encouraging a separative splitting-off tendency (the dangers of which we Protestants know, as well as the importance), which is frequently more than justified, but which must be combined with a farseeing responsibility for the unity and stability of the world; second, by drawing a line around the nation-state and

16

making *that* the *supreme object of its loyalty, devotion, and obedience.* I think it may be said without exaggeration that there never has been so widespread a recognition as now that a world order cannot be built out of seventy "sovereign" states, each one of which is actuated by a complete and avowed, and not only shameless but actually boastful, state egoism—each for itself alone. Here, for example, is Mr. W. Friedmann, in *The Crisis of the National State,* writing on the crisis which results from bringing into the twentieth century the notion of indefeasible and final sovereignty, internal and external, as set up by the Peace of Westphalia in 1648, conjoined with a doctrine of the "nation" which made it a culturally homogeneous pool of humanity, of which Europe presents hundreds of instances. It lies, he believes, in the very idea of national sovereignty that war *must* be the arbiter of disputes. While it may be doubted whether every national state, big and little, claiming to be sovereign, does accept the issue of war as the real test (since it would thereby invite its own collapse), the fact remains that the theory of sovereignty allows for no systematic method of settling disputes which can replace war. It simply has a mental blank on the subject. And such a method, the coming world order must find. And it is quite true, as Mr. Friedmann argues, that a system of collective security which any member can refuse to support at any time, as involved in the League's rule of unanimity, is too deferential to this essentially mischievous principle of sovereignty. We must replace that principle before any working international order can be set up.

Once this negative insight is gained, the positive insight comes swiftly after it. The world will not get a working international order unless and until it can find an object of loyalty, devotion, and obedience which *transcends the national state.* That is why it turns with a new and almost wistful deference to the church, asking, "What have *you* got along this line?" Well, what have we? That is the subject of the present paper.

THE DIFFICULTY OF THE PROBLEM

There is no profit in a type of encouragement which consists in pretending that the problems of world order are less difficult than they really are.

If there is hopefulness in the situation of the church today it is because it is disposed to know the worst, the only possible preparation for going on to a second stage of power in coping with the international situation.

There is a point of view from which world order appears quite simple: that of the analogy between a society of states and a society of persons. There are rights of persons: there are also rights of nations. If persons have a right to life, liberty, equality, property, so nations have a right to exist, to be self-determining, to have an equal voice in questions of justice, and to be secure in their national domains. This was the basis of a document put out in 1916 by the American Institute of International Law, entitled *A Declaration of the Rights of Nations.* It is also the point

of view of the liberal statesmanship of the nineteenth
century, during which Great Britain favored the independent statehood of modern Greece and modern Italy
on the ground of the principle of nationalism as it
was then seen.

But the difficulty is that the analogy is defective.
Nations are far more unlike among themselves than
are the persons of any one state. Think of Russia
and Switzerland, Germany and Denmark, the United
States and Panama, Brazil and Uruguay. They are
immovable as persons are not: they occupy the whole
world space so that there is no room for new ones;
they do not naturally die, nor are new ones naturally
born—perhaps a fortunate pair of conditions. But
further, they *can* change their outlines by addition
and subtraction as individuals cannot. The map of
Europe each hundred years is materially different
from its predecessor, and yet it is the same Europe.
State outlines, from one point of view, are extremely
important—consider the Soviet-Polish issue—and
from another, so plastic and variable that they seem,
over centuries, extremely unimportant. Such questions simply do not arise between citizens of a state.
Hence there is no background of legal analogy for
dealing with them. Yet it is just such questions that
drag mankind into wars.

In domestic matters, the aggressor is always wrong,
because there are ethical or legal means of dealing
with any issue for which a man might resort to force.
In international matters we can only say the presumption is against the aggressor. We should like to say

19

the aggressor is always wrong, but we can say that only when we know that there are adequate ethical or legal methods of dealing with his particular problem which he is willing to accept as just.

Unless we are prepared to say that it is always just to leave things the way they are, and therefore always unjust to change them, we face the as yet unsolved problem of defining what is a just apportionment of the earth among the nations. The absence of a rational solution to this problem is the chief reason why Germany turned toward the Nazi theory of state will. They saw the rosy optimism of England as the faith of a people, well satisfied, and willing to bless the *status quo* as just.

Another reason why the problem of world order is less simple than it appears to be is that there are *two kinds* of self-assertion among nations which are harmful to others, the brutal and the polite. The brutal gangster arouses instant condemnation and incites the threatened world against him. The polite gangster may pass for a good citizen of the world community unless you happen to be in his path.

For example, there are ways of using financial power, when weaker powers are in need of credit, so as to increase an already great advantage and prevent competitors, in what appears to be an open market, from securing a footing. The polite gangster succeeds by his wit and maintains respectability. A stable world order must secure itself equally against both kinds of wrong. Religion can play no favorites in a

20

FAITH AND WORLD ORDER

problem of this kind, but it is bound to see where the obstacles lie, the hidden as well as the open and notorious.

Perhaps the main point, however, which one ought to make in speaking of the difficulties is the strong psychological ground for the national spirit.

There is a general rule of human society to the effect that the *smaller groups tend to absorb the loyalties needed by the greater groups* to make them work. When Wilson was president of Princeton he waged war against the fraternities because these more intimate associations occupied their members to the detriment of their loyalty to the college. But Wilson was fighting a deep-rooted trouble. The family, as a small group, tends to absorb *its* members and especially at the beginning to make them such poor citizens that they are sent off on a honeymoon until they can recover their sense of proportion.

Every state has feared, and many states have suppressed, their secret clubs and societies. After the French Revolution, England waged a housecleaning campaign against groups which met and talked politics in taverns, and it was long before it felt comfortable about dissenting churches and trades unions. The intensest loyalty will go to the group in which a man feels most at home. Every man wants to belong to something greater than himself. His social self, which is as a rule his nobler self, requires to breathe in, and give itself for, a being which has a wider outlook than his own, and a longer span of life. But he cannot give this warmth and devotion to many. Plato thought he

21

must diminish the lure of the family to enhance the bond of his republic. But if men thus give their concrete affections first to their families and then to their states, what have they left for a superstate or an international organization? It is the very strength and spirituality of the nation which make it a natural concentration for such loyalty as a man can feel for the sources of his orderly community life. It is not an evil psychology but a good psychology to which the international community, the world order, has had to subordinate itself.

Further, all these loyalties gain part of their strength from contrast. You care for your own family just because it is not any other family. You care for your nation because it differs from every other nation, and you choose it. But the world community is in contrast with *nothing;* it has no outside and therefore represents no choice.

The world community does not at the moment represent a *cause* which needs to be promoted. The human mind is always in search of a cause to which it can give itself. This requires an active agent within an environment. The world as a whole furnishes an environment to internal groups but it has no environment of its own.

Now national empires are large groups intermediate between the nation and the world. The British Empire, as the largest and most coherent of these groups, represents for its British membership a concrete *cause*. The British Empire, as Britons think of it, has something to *do* in the world. In London, in 1931, as

22

I was leaving for the Far East on a study of Christian missions, I was told by a retired member of the British civil service that missions were all very well, but the real agency for civilization in the world was the British Empire; it was worth "all the missions put together." Now I do not subscribe to this opinion, but I understand it; and there is enough in it to make it understandable to us. The British Empire *has* promoted civilization. And one can understand, too, why our British allies, in considering the reforms which are to come out of the war, have directed their attention first of all to the internal reform of England, and then to new interpretations of colonial policy *within the Empire*. This has tended to be the limit of their concern for a better world. The empire has tended to absorb whatever of loyalty and interest their members have for a concrete cause beyond the state.

The German people have conceived a somewhat similar ideal. They call it the *Grosslebensraum*. It is a group of states large enough to be self-sufficient in the economic sense; and some writers, including Mr. Friedmann, have accepted this as perhaps the best arrangement for the world, dividing the whole world into a few, perhaps half a dozen, wide areas which would absorb, on some basis of consent, the smaller nations.

Now we have no reason to decry or disparage the enthusiastic devotion of the British or German or French citizens to these larger conceptions (apart from the way they propose to establish them). The British Empire, in particular, has a glamour. It has had a noble history. Yet I can see also that absorption

23

of loyalty by these wider conceptions is one of the serious problems which any new world order has to face. I say nothing here of their internal abuses, which are inherent in the form of empire, but point out solely that because of their grandeur of conception they impede the higher loyalty even more than does the national state.

THE RESOURCES FOR WORLD ORDER APART FROM FAITH

By a world in order we do not mean a world in which there is no trouble, but a world in which the trouble that arises can be met and settled without throwing the whole into turmoil. In all families, I am told, there are troubles, in the sense that there are issues of policy. But a family is called "disorderly" only if such issues reach the point of physical violence or disturbance of the neighbors. The essence of social order is the existence of *a means for decisive settlement.* And for this, there are three available resources in the world community, apart from faith; namely, *force, authority,* and *law.* We shall look for a moment at each of these.

1. *Force.* The word "power" is not one from which Christians ought to shrink. Power, in physics, is capacity to do work. This capacity is morally neutral; but one might argue that if one *can* have capacity to do work, it is both idle and immoral *not* to have it. The state, as a vast concentration of the powers of individuals, has something to do in the world, and so long as it sticks to its legitimate job, it cannot have

24

too much power. We must always thank God for power, as the opposite of impotence and frustration.

Now an order based on force may have the qualities of prompt and final decision. The potential disturbers of world peace, no matter what their motives, will be driven to peaceful methods of attaining their objects if an umpire is available with sufficient power to make the challenging of its decision imprudent.

There are obvious objections to a world order based solely on power, if there could be such a thing. First, is the matter of justice. If the settling power is genuinely disinterested, its settlements would approximate justice, solely because it is human, and justice tends toward peace. But powers great enough to keep the world quiet by main force could never be disinterested. Such power always acts so as to increase its own control, or at least not to diminish it. And the self-perpetuation of dominant power is not, as a rule, to the long-distance benefit of mankind, chiefly because of the lack of perfect wisdom on the part of any fixed grouping.

2. *Authority.* There is a disposition in men to refer their actions to a habitual source of authority. They are open to suggestions from that source as from no other. Within the state, a government which can claim the title "legitimate," even though it is the legitimacy of a hereditary house, can command a certain obedience on the part of those who accept that line, quite apart from its power, and often apart from its actual ability or worth. The presumption of such obedience is that the legitimate government has a cer-

25

tain spiritual fitness, for which there is no substitute on the part of rivals, who might show greater material efficiency. In fact, authority is essentially a *moral* bond. The prestige of the Supreme Court of the United States is due not alone to high-level ability, but also to the tradition of moral responsibility which that bench has maintained through a long period of years.

But how can a world order be based on authority? There is no legitimate rule, for there is no world ruler; there is no weighty Supreme Court; there is no panel of great publicists giving authoritative interpretations of international issues. Nevertheless, I dare say that the conduct of states has always been influenced by a type of judgment we might fairly call authoritative. We remember that the authors of our own Declaration of Independence thought they ought not to proceed to the radical deed of separation without due "respect to the opinions of mankind." They assumed that there was such a thing as a public opinion of the civilized world in regard to such disturbing actions; they knew that the new state would require the intangible which business calls "good will"; they respected what has sometimes been called "the verdict of history." And vague as that phrase may be, it is quite clear that every world disturber is troubled by the reality behind it and endeavors to set up through his speeches a reasoned justification of his course.

Now this vague authority is felt in the rise or fall of the reputation which individual states enjoy for fair dealing, keeping their treaties, paying their debts. It is also a part of the prestige which is sometimes credited solely to power. For behind the power of great states, there is felt to be an element of reason, in so far as political and military power testify to cultural and scientific advance, and to whatever moral qualities are evidenced in the political solidarity of large populations. Since men are never governed by fear and force alone, but always in part by conviction and loyalty, no state, modern or ancient, can be a great power unless it is also in some degree a spiritual fabric; and if it adds to its present cohesion a century-long durability, it will enjoy a position in the international field of moral weight not at all identical with nor limited to its striking force. And this authority will be all the more impressive because there are no international organs to make that authority compulsive.

It is for this reason that the League of Nations, in its origin, decided to make its chief reliance its appeal to public opinion and not an appeal to power; advocates of a "League to Enforce Peace" put their case in vain. A series of wise decisions would have built up, by degrees, a moral authority which would have strengthened its position and rendered further decisions more effective. It could not at once bring to bear on political problems even such wisdom as it had, because the prestige which would have made its judgments effective has to be a product of time.

I judge therefore that a world order based on authority is at least possible. Whatever institution takes the place of the League will have to depend on authority, rather than on power, if, as I certainly trust may be the case, there is no world government endowed with preponderant power. The difficulty with such an institution is primarily, again, the self-interest of great states, which makes them biased judges in their own case. Their moral weight may be high when they can serve as true umpires, and very low when their own interests are involved. And an institution whose policies were governed chiefly by a group of great powers would be suspect from the start. It would have to win its authority by a strict regard for an independent source of judgment. Such a source, in domestic matters, is the law. What value can this factor have in international affairs?

3. *Law.* Where law is known and accepted, human behavior is stabilized. Quite apart from a written law, every human being lives according to an inner law of some sort, because he will always produce some kind of reason to justify his conduct. (If you doubt this, just try to go through a single day on the fixed principle of not having any reason for what you do, so that the proper reply to every question of, "Why did you do that?" should be, "For no reason, but because I chose to.") But the reasonings of different persons do not coincide, nor the judgments of the same judge on different occasions—unless there is *an announced rule* on which dependence can be placed. A community composed entirely of men disposed to be reasonable, but not under law, would differ from that same community under law, by the important circum-

stance that in the latter each citizen would know what
to expect from the others in the ground covered by the
law.

If these divergent opinions about what is reasonable
could thus be reduced to one, then the law in such a
community would need no other legislative or enforc-
ing agency. For the desire to be rational is insep-
arable from human nature.

Why should this principle not also apply to a community of nations? This was certainly in the mind of
those seventeenth century jurists who so hopefully
drew up the outlines of a system of international law.
If there is a right and a wrong for individual action,
why is there not also a right and a wrong for state action?

The question was natural, and the dreams of men
from that day to the period following Versailles have
been governed by it. But one of the great obstacles
to the success of that law was born about the same
time, the theory of the sovereignty of the nation-state,
which we have already encountered. The state must
be the source of law, and in that sense the creator of
legal obligation; but no law can bind such an author of
law. It must be in a strict sense, "above the law."
On this theory, international law can have no force
beyond the free consent of the several states to abide
by it; if this consent is not given, at any point, there
is nothing over the sovereign state to compel its obedience, or to make it a duty.

But one reason why the principle of sovereignty has
been so insisted upon is just the point we touched on

at the beginning—the many ways in which a group of nations is *unlike a group of persons,* so that the whole attempt to transfer the rights of men to the rights of nations is in danger of breaking down. Let me give an example or two.

During the last war there were a number of very intelligent people in this country who retained their German citizenship and who thought that we were taking the events of that war too much from the legal and ethical point of view. One of them said to me: "You Americans are making a mistake. This war is not over a moral issue. The issue is this: Here are the Germanic peoples, multiplying in number and in strength and pressing eastward. At the same time the Slavic peoples are multiplying in number and strength and are pressing westward. At some time a clash was bound to occur. But surely you cannot say that the increase of populations is a moral issue."

This plea by no means disposes of the moral issue which presents itself in every modern war; but it does indicate one root of war for which there are no exact parallels in the relations between individuals. The natural growth of person A does not bring him into collision with the natural growth of person B, so that a contest is bound to arise in order to decide which one shall absorb, dominate, or displace the other! And if such a situation should arise, by what rule of justice could a community decide whether to have one full-grown individual or two individuals, each permanently flattened on one side?

Or, consider the issue presented by the Panama
Canal project in the days of Theodore Roosevelt,
where the security of the United States was on one
side and the political integrity of a small nation on
the other. It is hard to say that there are differences
in the magnitude and importance of nations which
affect one's judgments of what is right; and it is
equally hard to say that there are not. But at least
this is clear, that there are no quite similar problems
in the cases which come before our civil courts. For
it is not a simple situation in which the great and the
small, the rich and the poor, stand on the same level
before the law; it is a situation in which the position
of one of the parties gives it a preponderant influence
on the peace of the world, and thus gives it responsibilities that reach far beyond its own borders.

I have mentioned the two great obstacles to the
very notion of a community of states governed by an
international law. I do not think that either one of
them is decisive.

As for the idea of sovereignty, that is, in substance,
purely a matter of definition, a useful legal convention, which is already yielding on many sides to the
many lines of interdependence which make the notion
of complete autonomy, law-unto-oneselfness, out of
drawing with the facts. The legal theory of sovereignty must be revised so that it shall not be destroyed by this increasing interaction. When this is
done, it becomes simply another name for final responsibility; there must be some identifiable executive, legislative, judicial body in each state whose

31

decisions can be taken as the decisions of that state. But the reason for this is obvious: it is in order that some definite agent *may be held accountable,* which is quite the reverse of any conception of sovereignty that makes it free from all accountability. And if the "sovereign" is simply the responsible decider, then, like other human moral agents, he becomes subject to the superior law that he must keep his promises (*pacta sunt servanda*), pay his debts, refrain from injuring his neighbors, and carry out the duties of a respectable state in regard to keeping order at home and giving his own citizens the basic rights of man. These points are the basic principles of international law.

The second obstacle is more serious. But the difficulty of the questions raised under the "nonjusticiable" title does not mean that they are to be determined by arbitrary will. The basic rights to be affected are not the rights of nations, but the rights of the individuals in nations. However boundaries may be shifted, it is *the effect on individual human lives that matters.* There must therefore be such a thing, in each case, as a "reasonable" decision, as distinct from any result reached by appeal to force. And where there is reason, there is already the possibility of law.

The idea of a world order based on law, therefore, is one which the human race cannot give up, and which ought to be a main object of the foreign policy of our own country.

But all law is weak unless there is something beyond it as a source of obligation. Specific laws are weak because they are changeable. No one of them is "the" eternal law. The more completely international law is codified, the less permanent will any one of its articles be. What men have formulated, they can reformulate. International statutes or precepts will for many years lack the prestige of rules sanctioned by long and widespread usage and confirmed by a series of decisions of an international court. And finally, every system of law is weak in the respect that it cannot *generate the emotion* which will hold nations to its observance when it contravenes their momentary interest. It is especially for this final reason that a world order based on law *must be supplemented by a world order based on faith.*

To summarize the situation, our resources for world order add up in some such way as this:

No one of these three is ever relied on alone, though there are theorists who try to rely on power alone; in fact, they all cooperate. Power requires authority to give it any sort of moral quality, without which it disintegrates. Authority requires law to give it justice in its temper and world-wide acceptance. But law, weakest of all secular resources, requires faith—weaker still, from the secular point of view—to launch it into effectiveness as the spirit of a working community. Apart from faith, the whole pyramid loses its inner harmony and sense, and therefore its vitality. It tends to become an inconsistent mixture of power politics mitigated by fragments of morality out of place.

The question is whether religious faith is in a position in the world today to make this whole setup a living unity.

WHAT ARE THE RESOURCES OF FAITH?

On November 11, 1931, there was dedicated a new Buddhist temple at Sarnath, in the Deer Park in which Buddha was supposed to have preached his first sermon. This event was a notable one in the return wave, on which Buddhism is coming back into India, from which it had practically vanished several centuries ago. It was made notable by two special circumstances, a gift of relics of the Buddha, presented by the British Government of India, and a speech by Narendra Nath Das Gupta, head of the Sanskrit College in Calcutta, and in that capacity a prominent member of that Hindu community which had formerly been most influential in the expulsion of Buddhism from its native land. In this speech, Pundit Das Gupta made, in effect, the following concluding statements:

> Christianity has failed in Europe to prevent Christian nations from attacking one another in deadly combat, though for centuries it has preached there a gospel of peace and good will. Buddhism has actually promoted peace on the continent of Asia. It has never spread itself by means of force nor by the use of methods of com-

pulsion. It has brought a genuine fraternity
among the lands to which it has spread. I therefore welcome this event, which symbolizes a mile-
stone in the march of the future Hindu-Buddhist
culture of Asia.

At the time of this speech, Das Gupta's statements
were approximately true, though Japan had already
struck in Manchuria. The ideal of a Hindu-Buddhist
culture rather than a Christian culture for Asia was
alluring, plausible, and, to the Christian conscience,
a problem requiring thought.

It indicated, among other things, the belief of Das
Gupta that the problems of world order were at bottom problems of religious faith and that there existed
in Asia the promise of sufficient unity on this matter
to give reasonable ground for hope.

Since that time, the Buddhist world has split asun-
der by the widening of the breach made in September of 1931. Japan, the most actively Buddhist of
any Asiatic power (though not the most exclusively
Buddhist), has made herself the political enemy of
China, the potential enemy of India, and the absorber,
under the pretense of friendship, of the other Buddhist lands of Southeastern Asia. What we can say
on behalf of Buddhism is that the Japanese policy
seems less dictated by Buddhism than by Shinto, so
far as it has a religious basis at all. But in Japan,
two of the leading sects of Buddhism are deliberately
pugnacious in their spirit; and the Goddess of Mercy,
Kwannon, has been pressed into service as the divine
patroness of the Asiatic campaign. To this extent,

it has taken the mold of official Shinto, the nature of whose faith contains the prophecy of the present conflict.

In a temple of the Tenrikyo sect of Shinto near Nara, Japan, there is an important brass plate in the middle of the floor. This plate marks a place memorable in the history of the universe, for directly under it, the sun-goddess began the creation of the earth. From this center, creation expanded to form the Japanese islands; then beyond a stretch of the primeval waters, the mainland of Asia was congealed. And after Asia, the rest of the earth. During my stay in Japan I never heard any discussion of the relation between symbol and literal truth in religious tradition and I am unable to say how many of the six million Tenrikyo adherents follow this myth as history, nor to how many of the rest of Japan the other similar myths of Shinto have a basis in fact. But as a symbol, it represents a wide belief that Japan is the radiant center from which enlightened government of the world must some day spread.

In judging this application of a religious outlook in Japan, there are certain things to be remembered. Many Japanese, including not a few Japanese Christians, continue to believe in the beneficent mission of their country. They are ignorant of the conduct of their soldiers in the field. They have no practical acquaintance of any kind with a political order based on freedom. Hence the note of faith in a divine structure of history, which must eventually govern human affairs, lacks any effective release from the nationalistic plan of promotion.

At the same time, this very fact testifies to the inherent weakness of Buddhism before the heavy strains of world politics. For had Buddhism offered an alternative way of promoting Japanese culture abroad, instead of falling in with the primitive state-craft of Shinto, the liberal elements within Japan would have had a more effective religious support.

It is true that Hinduism and Buddhism have never abetted war on their own initiative. But it is now evident that, being above the battle, they have not been able, any more than Christianity, to prevent it.

In its own nature, religious faith is universal; and, binding all men to the same spiritual source and goal, it creates a supernational fraternity, out of which a genuine world order can be born, and must some day be born. But all religion has proved itself, so far, ineffective to bring that day near. And we have to look at the reasons for that ineffectiveness.

The simple fact that we have many religions in the world, instead of one world faith, is itself one answer to the question. The very intensity of religious conviction and its supreme importance to the life of the individual have made the differences matters of vital import, so that in fact religious leaders have spent much energy in denouncing the errors of other religious leaders—and the colder world of politics has inclined to accept both sides as correct on this point. We shall later have something to say on this matter, but I doubt whether today it is as great an impediment as it was a generation ago. The reasons lie rather in the attitudes of different religions to the whole political situation of man. Of these attitudes, Buddhism and Shinto are typical.

There are two types of religions in respect to their effort to become universal. There are the religions originally identified with a particular group of mankind, such as Judaism, Hinduism, Shinto, which realize their universal mission by group diffusion or mastery. And there are religions universal in their very definition, which realize their universal mission by appeal to individual assent; such are Buddhism and Christianity. The obvious peril of the group mission is its political entanglement and its provincial outlook. The peril of the individual mission is its abstraction. Preaching the principle of love and the insignificance of race, sex, nation, in the eye of God, it runs the risk of discounting the true value of the dynamic human group and thus of losing influence over it.

The result of this dilemma is that the local type of faith tends to develop a universal faith, whose conquest can take place by individual assent. Let us call these the faiths of amiability. Islam gives rise to Bahaism; Hinduism, to the Ramakrishna variety of Vedanta. Judaism develops a liberal version which is hardly distinguishable from varieties of liberal Christianity: I have heard distinguished Jews, like the late Rabbi Voorsanger of California, say that Judaism and Unitarianism were practically identical in creed.

But all these faiths, or forms of faith, by definition universal, seem to share the same feebleness of political impact. Men do not unite for heavy work on the basis of the abstract man, but on the basis of the historic man and his issues, and his future.

If Christianity has an advantage in dealing with politics, it lies here. Judaism is historical, and in its history strong. But it has become too much the religion of "return," with an attachment in the past, seeking the "restoration" of Israel, the restoration of something that once was on the hill of Zion, and must be once more. Christianity, inheriting this valid historical trait, has broken with the past anchorage and has set its anchor in the future. It lives in the eternal, but in the moving eternal which is alive in time; it believes in the God-man, the God who is at work in the historical process, and who therefore summons his followers to redeem that process, and make it in its full sweep a movement toward a Kingdom of God on earth.

Further, as I think, Christianity has an inherent pugnacity of its own, rather stimulated than dashed by repeated failure. It is for that reason that I have a special word to offer to the Christian community of this country at this time.

The Program of Faith for World Order

There are various things which hearten us as we look around the world, even the disturbed and tragic world of our time, and one of these is the fact that nations as well as men are often better than their professions. There have been nations who through their monarchs have pretended to be concerned with nothing but the interests of their own state; there has never been such a state in fact. Much of the accusation of hypocrisy leveled against Great Britain is due to the fact that it has mingled morality with self-interest quite frequently, indeed almost regularly, and has then been naturally inclined to give the most laudable name to the mixture. This is far better than not having any mixture of morality at all. And the very fact that the ethical name has been chosen is a sign of the perennial power which the moral prejudices of the public exercise on the acts of statesmen. The more democratic a regime is, the more the conscience of men will carry over from private to public affairs and international affairs, even in defiance of the logic of the situation.

This indicates one principle of Christian statecraft; namely, the eternal *working from inside,* in the confidence that state egoism will be modified even when it cannot be finally cured. In the inner self-renewal, and the increased knowledge of international fact, lies the most immediate hope that foreign policies will be bent toward a world of just and durable peace. With this should go the following external objectives:

1. That all nations should be urged to provide in their constitutions for the effectiveness of the citizen's conscience on the acts of government as a factor in external peace. This means the adoption of at least one element of a democratic constitution whereby there is guaranteed not alone freedom of conscience,

but a channel for its political influence. In the nature of the principle of freedom, this cannot be an imposed requirement on any people, but it can be recommended by the inner strength of democracies themselves as they renew their own faith and duty.

2. A demand that the economic roots of world disorder be not concealed under the calls for political and ideological reform. Not that religious faith has competence in the economic sphere; but that it has an inalienable concern (a) in honesty and truth, and (b) in the living standards of man in all lands.

3. A demand that no human being, and no group or nation, be held as the property of any other human being or nation; but that every soul of man be respected in terms of his own capacity to grow and master his destiny. The principle of empire must be revised.

4. Unremitting pressure for an adequate setup for the principles of international law, revitalized and applied, with especial attention to the refractory questions of status.

5. Reconstruction of a league of nations on the principle of authority, backed by an instructed world opinion, in which the thought of the church shall play an increasingly vital role.

The inherent power of faith is that it directly undercuts the series of world envelopes with their diminishing intensities of loyalty.

Being world-wide, it is wider than the empire, but it is also more intimate.

It is the only power which directly commands by an inner and inescapable voice. We completely misrepresent it if we think of it as one wider sphere.

It has an inherent importance because it supplies the scale of importance. Hence it is always more powerful, if one listens at all, than the voice of national advantage, which is in many ways a pseudo voice.

The national entity has no intrinsic necessity as to its boundary.

The religious being has an intrinsic necessity in his relations to mankind. He cannot keep his faith with his Maker if he destroys his duty to his fellow man.

Confucius said, "He who offends the gods has no one to whom he can pray."

Christ said, in effect, "He who offends one of the least of these my brethren, has no one to whom he can pray." And men reach the time sooner or later when they realize that prayer is their breath of life, far beyond the political sphere in its necessity and its realism.

CULTURE AND PEACE

WILLIAM ERNEST HOCKING

A S A New Hampshire farmer, I have had occasion
to observe the working of the slow process of
bringing a stranger into a New England neighborhood.
If he comes into New Hampshire from as far away as
Vermont or Maine, he has to go through a period of
probation. There are two questions about him. One:
How does he take the peculiar difficulties of New
Hampshire life, the rocky and hilly farms, the local
crops and weeds, the hard roads, and the hard winters?
Two: What does he like? Can he talk our language?
How does he amuse himself? Can he join the neighbors in a barn dance, a husking bee, or a Grange meeting? He has to pass both examinations before he is
accepted. But the main thing is the quality and extent
of his cooperation. If he takes a good and straight-
forward part in community enterprises, the neighbors
will stand from him even a certain amount of good-
humored criticism of those skinny cattle that earn
their living on the mountainsides and look (as one
Vermonter put it) "as though they all hed tuber-
clusis." And naturally, as these enterprises are numerous, the opportunities for acquaintance through
common work multiply. I think it may fairly be said
that no two people are well-grounded friends until
they have done some hard work together. Of course,
no one is a wholly comfortable fellow townsman until

he also knows the local gossip and is seen to be free from meanness and to be understanding in his judgment of frailty.

It comes down to this: Do you worship the same gods that we do, and do you suffer under the same sorts of sin that we do, which impede your effort to do your worship worthily? I use the word "gods" in the plural in order to cover the field of what we mean by "culture," the things which appeal to us as good, as beautiful, and as true.

Now I think that, in principle, the social problem of harmony in the world community follows the same pattern. Nations do not move into one another's neighborhood; the neighborhood of all nations moves outward, as the world shrinks, and takes the formerly distant members in. They cannot escape if they would, nor can they be expelled. By being on the planet, they are born into the world community; and their citizenship in any world organization should be as automatic as the citizenship of an infant born in the United States. There should be no such thing as joining or resigning from the new league of nations.

But whether they are welcome or unwelcome, comfortable or uncomfortable depends, as in the case of the New England village, on the nature of their complaints, on the quality of their cooperation, and on their wise sharing in the moral problem of world order. The ultimate question for any such member is, *Does that member worship the same gods?*

This is why religion, in the past, has been so important a test of the possibility of neighborly relations.

The forcible conversion of the Germanic tribes was not a matter of pure and ruthless violence in the spiritual world. It was a rude test of whether these tribes could see what had become for their spiritual masters the focus of all culture. If they could see it, all other cooperation could follow; if they could not see it, all other cooperation would be hollow and devoid of common sense. There is a defensible logic in this point of view. If Japan should become mistress of the world, she would want to make it a Shinto world; Shinto has been fitting itself out as a universal religion rather than as a local Japanese religion with that role in mind; and Shinto missionaries have made their way to California, to Germany, and to other places in the Western World. On the Asiatic Continent, Japan would probably use the prevalence of Buddhism as a bond of spiritual union and introduce by degrees the Shintoized varieties of Buddhism which have developed in Japan.

When Islam was engaged in its career of world conquest, it showed a similar sense of the necessity of a common religious outlook, but with a definite range of toleration. Christianity and Judaism were its kindred; all three had the same Bible as the basic religious literature. They were all, therefore, "religions of the Book." The Koran, as the latest revelation of God, contained and absorbed the truth of the earlier. But these three could understand one another. Other religions presented serious barriers and had to pass the more rigorous test: "Can they see what we see? If not, cooperation in cultural matters is a mockery."

45

Nothing in the history of mankind is more remarkable, in view of this attitude, than the respect and rapid appreciation with which the armies of Islam approached the cities and works of learning and art of the Near East—an almost uncultured folk suddenly finding itself military master of an ancient classical civilization, then under Christian government. They might have destroyed it all, as they did some parts of it, in view of this logical religious test. Instead of this, they absorbed it. They saw the beauty of Damascus, and *camped outside* the walls! They saw the beauty of the great Church of Saint John, and divided the use of it with the Christian congregation! They saw the wonder of Greek literature and philosophy, learned their Plato and Aristotle by heart, as they did their Koran, wrote learned commentaries on them both, and kept them safe for centuries until Europe was ready to receive them. They showed that the spirit of Islam had a great cultural hospitality, even beyond the scope of the "religions of the Book." But it was still the religious insight which framed it all in.

Meanwhile, we in Europe had but one word for the Saracen. He was the "infidel"; and in time we felt bound to rescue the Holy Sepulcher from his polluting grasp. He could tolerate us, but we could not tolerate him. We could not understand a world comity in which anything but the Christian faith furnished the deep-lying medium of understanding: men must worship the same gods if they would live together in understanding, and these gods must be aspects of the one true God, the Christian Trinity. As the event proved, we could not oust the Saracen from the world; we could only locally clear the ground of his influence; and since he was then ahead of us in civilization, the culture of the world received contributions from both spheres, and from the Jewish element which interpenetrated both and served to a certain extent as an interpreter.

Now what has happened since these days in which it seemed an axiom that the limits of religious agreement are at the same time the limits of cultural understanding?

SECULARIZATION AS A CONTRIBUTION TO PEACE

The great thing that has happened is the *secularization of culture in Europe,* as it has not been secularized anywhere else in the world. Science and the arts have found their own methods and their own voices and are building up their cumulative treasures almost as if religion were not in the same community. If they are intrinsically world-wide in their reach, they have become world-wide without asking the permission of any religious authority.

Science spreads, not because it is a part of Christian culture but because it is intrinsically human. It is, as Bacon apprehended, for all those who can observe and think; and since all men are endowed with similar eyes and similar brains, all men everywhere can, if they will, test and verify the results of Western science and make them their own. The democracy of science lies not in the fact that all men are equally endowed with scientific capacity, either to discover or

47

to understand, but in the fact that science offers no obstacles to anybody except those that lie in the nature of its subject matter. One need not be a Christian to contribute to a science which Christian Europe has developed. The Japanese biologists and the Hindu physicists have an equal right in those temples. And through such cooperation, one sees the fabric of a world culture being spun, which is at the same time an element in world understanding.

I have often marveled at the rapid spread of science in recent years into all parts of the world and at the fraternity of scientific men which it has brought about. Science is not propagated by any promoting agency; it is sought and carried away by generations of students, who transplant its spirit and begin its work on new soils, in a manner similar to that of the runners of a strawberry plant! No doubt a part of this zest is due to the theory that science is the secret of the strength of Western communities. But it is also due in part to the intrinsic joy of making one's way into a universal body of *truth*. It is the wholeness of truth itself which unites the minds who take part in its discovery.

And while science is not all of truth, nor truth the whole of culture, we cannot forget that Truth, in the broader sense, is one of the names of God, and that for Gandhi, God's nearest name is Truth. In this sense, all scientists worship the same god. And the requirements for his worship are severe, well-understood, and self-executing. No one can contribute to this truth without mastering the thought and the technique of those who have contributed before. A rigorous honesty in observation and report is the essence of the path to success. The fraternity of science is thus a *moral* fraternity; and its laws are susceptible neither of bribery nor of evasion. So far as it goes, it binds men in a unity of good faith.

Now the field of art is different from that of science. There is no such thing as a world formula for success in painting or sculpture, no such thing as a universal method of producing beauty, no accepted canon of what constitutes good music. Art has a rooted localism, in which the difference seems at times to outweigh the resemblance.

In 1900 I experienced a premonition of things to come in this field, without knowing at the time how prophetic the event was. I was returning from England on a cattle ship. I had gone over on that same ship with a number of fellow students to visit the World's Fair at Paris. We worked our way over; we were free riders on the return journey. Among our fellow passengers was a young Japanese student of art. He had been working in the studios of Paris and was returning via America to Japan. I fell into conversation with him. He was mildly appreciative of French art; but his summary judgment of all the art of Europe was negative. "I am going home," he said, "to tell my people to continue in their own traditions of painting and to stop imitating this shallow and heartless art of Europe, which only depicts surfaces and has, in the long run, no substance, no mean-

49

ing.'' This student was certainly not convinced that all artists worship the same gods.

There is a rough resemblance between art and language; indeed language as an assemblage of symbols may be regarded as a collective and fluent work of art. We expect languages to mold themselves directly on the emotional flow of a people's life, and so to vary instantly as we pass the border between one national temperament and another. We expect the art forms to change in the same instant. For—to put the matter the other way around—art is also a language. If it conveys nature, it conveys at the same time *the way someone feels* about that bit of nature, and this emotional tone will have its local quality. Art may be expected to separate mankind.

But this is not inconsistent with also uniting it, if, perchance, we wish the world to be qualitatively diverse. We expect, if we are sensible, to be puzzled by Chinese and Indian music, and to be baffled as well as fascinated by the intricacies of Buddhist iconography in India and Tibet. But we know by a certain stroke of command in the attack which such objects make on our minds and senses that here is a certain greatness of aesthetic speech. And in the higher reaches of that foreign tongue there come accents which we recognize directly; for all great art has its altitudes in which the power of simplicity fuses the message of beauty into syllables caught by an entire race. Our museums are not for nothing filled with pieces from the workshops of the Orient; and it is not for nothing that we regard the preservation of the noble works of Egypt, of Persia, and of China as being as important for the future of human culture as is the preservation of the works of Greece or of France. There are gods in these lands whom we do not know how to worship, some whose worship we look on with doubt; but there is a god of beauty whom Plato knew, and that god, under whatever name, has been worshiped by souls of every great civilization, still draws their people and other peoples toward him by way of those works of art, and thus brings unity across national and racial lines to those who perceive him.

Aesthetic theory has lagged in taking on a world scope. It has been cultivated by Western writers on Western and classic models. But through such writings as those of Laurence Binyon and of Lafcadio Hearn of Yanagi the supposed gulf is being crossed, and the aesthetics of the future will be a contemplation of the art work of a wider world, in principle universal. Even now, as Western art is running into lower levels of inspiration and seeking the sensational and discordant for lack of serious invention and from loss of the vein of veracity in which art must find its content, it turns for revitalization to the art of the East and, as my young Japanese shipmate of over forty years ago believed, will find there some secrets of eternal youth which we are in danger of losing.

If truth and beauty are intrinsically universal, so are goodness and the contrast of right and wrong. I shall not dwell on this, since I have done so elsewhere; but let me simply state that here, where relativity theorists have their favorite playground, showing from anthropology that "the mores can make anything right," just here history is proving them wrong. For law, which is the deposit of the human sense of justice, and which certainly has its local variations—law is becoming year by year a universal factor in social life. For the codes of Europe (the newer civil codes developed in Switzerland, Italy, Germany), having furnished models for similar codes in the newer states of the Near East and in South America, have also been used in drawing up codes for China, Japan, Siam. The general principles of law fit the conscience of men of all peoples. The specific statutes ought to vary in accord with the customs of the people, but they will vary, not in contradiction with the principles, but as the same principle is applied to different circumstances. The mores can *not* make everything right.

And while it is important for East and West to meet on lines of science and in a common admiration for works of art, it is far closer to the vein of international understanding that there should be agreement in moral sense, and therefore in law. For the judgment that East and West can never meet is chiefly grounded on an assumed moral difference. It is only the opposition of *ethical judgment* that puts an insuperable barrier between persons, and if this is elevated to a racial impasse, the outlook for the future of civilization would be dark indeed.

The Effect of This New Rapport on Religion

The cultural welding of the world into "One World" by the sharing of science, art, and law has had its effect on the idea of religion. If a secularized group of cultural interests like these has found its way to world scope without waiting for religion to catch up, there is one strong probability that has been created: namely, that religion is *more nearly one than it looks to be.*

For in spite of what we call secularization, which seems to mean that science and religion are completely independent, it remains the fact that if science is true science, and religion true religion, they do belong together. Religion is not identical with truth, but it *has* truth. And truth of all kinds and branches belongs together. So again with religion and art. Religion is not a mode of feeling; it is not a branch of aesthetics, though many people are held to it rather by its emotional appeal than by its doctrinal truth. Religion is not beauty; but it *has* beauty, and the religious note remains an ingredient of the highest beauty. Where art forgets this, it flattens out; and like much art that calls itself "modern," its search for dissonance and sensationalism is a confession of its loss of soul and so of substance. Hence if art has a universal element, so must religion. In brief, these cultural interests have strongly suggested that there is *already a world religion,* if we could but see it. It can do little to unify the race unless it can be made to appear; for so long

53

as men *think* they are worshiping different gods, it does not unify them to assure them that they are mistaken.

I believe it can be shown that a world religion does exist. And perhaps many of us are already convinced of it, so that I shall be saying things well known to them. If so, I ask them to bear with me while I speak to others among you who may believe I am wrong.

It will be agreed that under different names all religions worship God. It is not agreed that this is an important fact, since the different conceptions of God are just what make the obstacle between one creed and another. If (as a missionary friend of mine in Cairo maintains) the Moslem God is a God of power and the Christian God a God of love, the significant thing is not that both bow down to a supreme spiritual Being, but that one serves power and the other love. Professor Whitehead regards the great moment in religious history as that moment in which first the Hebrew prophets, then the great Greek thinkers Plato and Aristotle, then Jesus, proclaimed that God works by persuasion and not by force; for this reason, he regards the later moment at which Christianity became the official religion of Rome, and God became conceived, after the fashion of Caesar, as the divine and omnipotent ruler as a fatal moment in the history of the church, obscuring the purity of the Christian idea. About such views as this, there are several things to be said.

1. No religion worships pure power. The Moslem Allah is "the Merciful, the Compassionate."

54

2. No religion can omit the element of power from its conception of God; for God is the Being on whom we depend, and we cannot depend on a Being who has no power to sustain.

3. The issue between power and love, overdrawn as it is, still leaves a great realm of agreement in the idea of God. For all the ideas of God give him a definite relation to human obligation; he is the Will or Law which is above every human law, the Spirit who is most real and whom it is our first duty and happiness to obey. No religion could be a religion without offering men a scale of values and defining what is the most important of all goods, in view of their total destiny.

Now this is also the most significant contribution of religion to the international order.

For the main thing to be achieved is that men shall bring the perspective of a superhuman duty into their conduct of worldly affairs. This at once breaks the hard case of national self-sufficiency and of the false conception of sovereignty which makes each nation-state a supreme law to itself. If the peoples of the world can be brought into unity in the rejection of this false god—for that is just what sovereignty, so conceived, amounts to—the greatest step in the way of world peace will have been taken. For then it will become true, in a practical and substantial sense, that *all men worship the same god,* within the limits of that part of his definition.

It remains true that there are many differences in the conception of God which are important. I do not

55

believe that all ideas about God are true ideas. There are some which exclude others. The Moslem idea of the ineffable unity of God excludes all notions of plurality, whether Trinitarian or polytheistic. The Moslem is repelled alike by the Christian notion of Incarnation and the Hindu notion of the manifold apparitions of God in nature. There are issues here in which somebody is right and somebody is wrong, and until they become clear where the truth lies, men will continue to be divided.

But even here, there is a strong aid toward the discovery of common ground which comes from the side of science itself. The science of psychology, as applied to religious concepts, is showing itself able to say what religious doctrines mean in terms of religious experience and has often found common ground where there appeared to be unbridgeable gulfs. Let me give an illustration or two of this process.

1. *Hindu polytheism.* We cannot forget that Hinduism has given us, in the Vedanta, probably the strictest notion of the absolute unity of God that the race has achieved. The multiplicity of Gods, when one examines carefully what the word "god" means to the Hindu worshiper, has no resemblance to the ancient Persian or Greek polytheism. What they mean is that the *one* God has various ways of becoming perceptible to man's dull vision. Just as not all nature is beautiful to our eyes, but random spots here and there; just as not every mountain strikes our mind with the sense of sublimity; so not every being in the world rouses in us the sense of awe and wonder, perhaps of a touch

of holiness. The Hindu cherishes these suggestions
of the divine, makes images of them, tries to recall
them as a part of his worship. But he knows that in
all of these experiences it is the One, it is He, to whom
their thoughts must fly. Their polytheism—though
often degraded, and run into superstitious molds—
means in essence that God manifests himself everywhere, if we have eyes to see; in all events it is his
hand that guides us.

And there is no issue between Hindu and Moslem on
this point. For even more literally than in the usual
Christian thought, the good Moslem believes that "the
very hairs of your head are all numbered." These
thoughts certainly diminish the distance between the
three faiths. They certainly do not obliterate all the
differences. They add to the common ground on
which men can feel agreement in the object of their
supreme loyalty.

2. *The Bodhisattva and the Second Coming.* As another example, let me relate an incident which took
place in a Buddhist temple near Colombo in Ceylon
some years ago. A group of us were in Colombo waiting for our ship to Hong Kong. Having a free after-
noon, we decided to visit the temple of the Sleeping
Buddha some seven miles distant. Two of us found
ourselves, together with a priest, in the hall contain-
ing the heroic recumbent image when a woman came
in with an offering. She knelt in prayer, not before
the Buddha, but before a smaller standing image at
his feet.

I asked the priest, "Do your people pray to the Buddha?" "No," he said, "the Buddha is in nirvana. He is no longer aware of us. He would not hear our prayers."

"To whom do you pray?"

"We pray to the Bodhisattva, the Buddha to come. The Bodhisattva is now within the universe, we do not know where; but he hears our prayers and cares for us. He will some day be born in the earth."

"What will he do then?"

"He will bring men back to the truth from which they have wandered. He will bring peace to men and love."

At this point, my companion, a good Baptist, took part in the conversation. He asked: "What does this coming of the Bodhisattva mean to you?"

The face of the priest lighted up. "I long for his coming. I pray for his coming."

Then my companion said, "And I join in your prayer."

This remark, which I confess surprised as well as moved me, implied a stroke of recognition, not of identity, but of something important in common between the hope of the Ceylonese Buddhist and the hope of the Christian.

Now I suggest that the future peace of the world, which will have to be won and kept by severe effort— which will not happen by itself—can be promoted by whatever efforts we can today make to *discern and enlarge these areas of agreement,* which are far more important than is generally realized. The sense of fellowship in spiritual matters may be a mere idle sentiment, a wallowing in easy-minded amiability, hospitality of mind, a slightly more affirmative variety of the vice of "toleration." Anyone who brushes differences aside as insignificant is doing mankind no service; for the only thing in which men can ultimately unite is the truth. But the only way to find out where the differences lie is to become clear about the places where they do not lie. To say that the God of Islam is a God of power while the Christian God is a God of love is simply to misstate the issue and to create an endless amount of unnecessary dissension. No one should be afraid of an honorable and generous recognition of the great agreements that already exist.

And above all, let us never be afraid of those instantaneous human impulses in which kinship of spirit makes itself felt across lines of race and creed, those friendly intuitions which run from person to person, and mean: "I perceive in you one who does, under whatever name, worship the gods whom I also worship." For it is these human ties which furnish the motive power for the discovery of the agreements in meaning. The direct confidence of one person in another is a silken thread which can pull a rope, then a cable, then a bridge, on which the traffic of mankind can pass and repass.

THE LEVEL OF COMMON TASKS

I have spoken of the common goods, the ideas and ideals which men serve and may serve together. These are the quickest way to create unity; for by adding to truth or beauty one adds to the riches of all humanity at a single stroke. An idea is the one thing which affects billions of men with the same ease as one man.

But when, and in so far as, agreements exist, common enterprises can be undertaken. And a definite common task creates a sort of body for the common soul. Agreement in spirit always desires to become agreement in work. And vice versa, even when agreement in spirit is undefined, to undertake a common job is one of the best ways of creating or enlarging the agreement of spirit.

Nothing is more characteristic of the present era in international relations than the growth of these common tasks, representing the growing recognition of the reality of "One World."

The International Postal Union is the oldest and best established of these. In 1939 it had seventy-two members. The Tele-communication Union brings sixty-eight states together. A treaty regarding the traffic in opium has sixty-eight adherents. Sixty-three states adhered to the statute for a Permanent Court of International Justice. A smaller number, but an important number, have collaborated in the work of the International Institute of Agriculture at Rome. And clustering around the work of the League, there were many cooperative enterprises which have shown an independent vitality, among which the International Labor Office is prominent.

Such tasks imply common standards of performance. If there are backward peoples—as there assuredly are —it is far less effective to be told by the "advanced"

that this is the case than for the "backward" to make
the observation for themselves in a spirit of good
will and candor. It is the job-to-be-done which judges
impersonally and without words where one stands in
the scale of efficiency. Cooperation offers a constant
incentive to make good, to do one's share well—as well
as any other. And the effort itself makes for mutual
respect.

I do not urge that we should strive to multiply
these common undertakings; they will make their own
need evident as the world contracts. I urge simply
that we welcome them, take part in them, as they appear; and that we use them to promote the spirit of
understanding.

COMPETITIVE AND NONCOMPETITIVE GOODS: THE EMERGENCE OF NEW DIFFERENCES

Those who believe that peace has to be made must
make use of cooperation as a means to that end. They
must not forget that cooperation is also a famous
breeder of strife. The common effort brings out latent differences of energy—the loafer, the slacker; of
scruple—the pretender, satisfied with a cheap and
showy job, the cheat; of opinion—as to how things
should be done; and of ambition—as to who should
have the credit for doing them, and who should boss
the job. Even the noblest of our social deeds, our
charities, are not immune from the marks of common
vanity, pushingness, jealousy, and conceit.

The very fact that two people do worship the same
gods *may make them antagonists rather than friends.*

Two lovers of some rare commodity, prints or old books, meeting at an auction, may find themselves deadly rivals just because they are completely at one in their tastes! Even if we could bring all mankind to a common mind regarding what is good and true, we should not have solved the problem of peace so long as that common mind is in pursuit of objects of which the supply is not enough to go around.

The goods of the spirit are noncompetitive. Your share of truth and friendship is not diminished by what you give to me. But material goods are competitive: A's gain is B's loss. And even the goods of the mind have their material conditions. Santayana, in his latest book, tells of a clever ruse by which he gained a share in a fellowship for foreign study which he expected a classmate to win. The glory of political communities is in their contributions to culture, the common wealth of mankind. But the development of these goods lays tribute on all the wealth which the world can offer, and thus has a competitive base.

The ignoring of this situation is one of the weaknesses of much liberal and Christian good intention. The urge to share what is good, which is another way of expressing love of one's neighbor, is universal among mankind; for in all noncompetitive goods, a shared pleasure is an enhanced pleasure. It is quite possible to feel subjectively that one loves all mankind before one has subjected this enthusiasm to the strains of day-by-day cooperation. I have no scorn for this overflowing and untested friendliness, this a priori good will which has borne no burdens, this love of man at a safe distance, this benevolent interest, on principle, in the struggles of China and India; it is the only possible expression for 90 per cent of our natural goodness of heart, the raw material out of which all further practical goodness is fashioned. But I cannot forget that it is *untried.* The good feeling of America toward China is now being tested by the direct mixing of Chinese and Americans in the hard conditions of China's desolated battle front; and the real problem of cooperation begins there. Will this close association beget warmer friendliness or mutual friction and difficulty? The real friendship is one which has gone through this baptism of fire and has come out stronger.

The old liberal assumption that we had only to know more of people of different kinds to love them as ourselves was somewhat deficient in its psychology. And the lesson of this for those who would create an active peace lies in the sterner discipline of their own feelings as they encounter the actual faults of humankind. We Americans are exuberantly friendly in our first attack; we are dishearteningly shallow in passing beyond this point to the mutual meeting of human defects in the friend and to the moral deepening of both which its correction requires. Our divorce record is a symptom of our degree of failure at this second stage of the battle of peace. The problems of keeping peace in the family and in the international arena are morally identical.

How important this warning is in the field of international relations may be seen in the fact that most of the great wars of recent years are *civil* wars, in the sense that they take place between peoples culturally much alike. Germany and Italy could not have challenged Great Britain had they not been at approximately the same level of technological development, sharing in a rapid give and take in the advancement of sciences and arts. They were already worshipers of the same gods, in terms of the cultural interests. Strife between brothers is traditionally most bitter. And so far as future war is concerned, it is only between cultural brothers that it can occur; for no people or combination of peoples which had not come along to the same command of natural resources and toolmaking could put up a contest against one another.

They fight because, in spite of all they have in common in terms of noncompetitive goods, they *have not solved the competitive question* at the base of the social structure, the economic insertion in the planetary soil which is the source of population, social division of labor, the elaboration of institutions, and the emergence of genius.

This being the case, the great problem for those who would earn their peace will not be solved by merely increasing the amount of mutual knowledge, the volume of interchange, and the density of agreement at the higher cultural levels. It must do this, and then it must give itself with a new dedication to the deadly problems of the limited natural base of human life and the struggle for existence among states constantly in touch with that limited base.

The Basic Competitive Problem: Legal Solutions and Living Solutions

It is naturally not in the scope of our topic today to go into these problems of competitive good. We shall do no more than indicate two contrasting lines of attack. None of these are hopeless problems, though they involve the most difficult and intractable of all future causes of change, the diverse rates of multiplication among the races of men and the consequent changes in demand upon the soil. They are *not hopeless,* because already the resources of economy are sufficient to maintain the entire race at a much higher living standard than the present average level. They *are difficult,* because no culture can be based on a subsistence standard of living, and no standard, so far reached, has been found too great, or great enough.

Now there are two ways of approach to these problems, each of which is derived from the common cultural wealth of the race. One is the legal approach, whose maxim is an ultimate equality of men in their claim on liberty and justice, including an access to the goods of common culture. This maxim, without which legal thinking could hardly proceed, applying directly to individuals, by that same sign, does not apply directly to states. For if a state of a hundred million people were made equal to a state of ten million, in terms of competitive goods, the individuals in the larger state would obviously be put at a disadvantage of one to ten. International law, as we shall see in our next lecture, has to meet this difficulty.

The second approach is by way of the clews furnished by the living interest of one human group in another, an interest which is enhanced by *difference* and which cares to preserve differences for their own sake. It thus tends to supplement the legal maxim of likeness or equality.

There is no form of interest in mankind more widespread than the interest of the traveler. Men want to travel primarily because other parts of the world are different from their own part, and this truth, which is almost too banal to put into words, is nevertheless a truth which much of our "One World" pressure not only forgets but tends to obliterate. All the great seaport cities the world over have by now become deadly similar. The traveler who had been reading Whitman's great poem, "Passage to India"—

Passage, O soul, to India!
Eclaircise the myths Asiatic, the primitive fables.
. . . .
O you temples fairer than lilies, pour'd over by
    the rising sun!
You too I welcome . . .
You too with joy I sing[1]

—such a traveler, getting off the ship at Bombay or Calcutta, knows that he is definitely *not in that India;* he is in a modern municipality which—except for human splotches here and there—might be anywhere; he is in Cosmopolis! The more we mix, share, increase the common stock, reveal our secrets of trade, the more

---

[1]From *Leaves of Grass,* by Walt Whitman. Copyright, 1924, by Doubleday, Doran & Co., Inc. Used by permission.

we rob the world of any traveler's interest. The determined traveler is driven to the interior of Asia or to the great forests or to the Himalayas or to the Poles in order to slake his thirst for the different.

Now the traveler who is nothing else is an idler, a type of person which we could most easily get on without. There are lands which professionally fatten on his surplus, and by this very act they falsify the natural attractiveness of their charms. The traveler by his existence ruins the thing he feeds on, both for himself and for all others. By great effort the Dutch Government tried to keep Bali a place unspoiled, but in time great steamers made it a port of call, and Bali became self-conscious, and its beauty and charm pass into memory.

But this idle interest is a symbol of something more profound, the respect for the different, which has its far-reaching message for the peace of the world.

It indicates that the various types of habitat, climate, geography, racial background, mental attitude, are intended to enrich the world, not throw it into strife. In the differences lies the promise of future fertility of imagination, of that serenity and poise which has no need to have been everywhere and know everything, but can reach dignity within a region which is its home. Unless there are deep-rooted men as well as broad-minded men—men identified with the harsh coasts of Labrador, the monasteries of Tibet, the pampas of the Argentine, the mountain farms of New Hampshire, and all the other wild, remote, and savagely individual corners of this small planet—the world runs the risk of getting sick of its own monotonous tricks of survival. We have a new art to learn, the art of making our neighbors proud of their idiosyncrasies, rather than ashamed of them. Isaiah Bowman, our distinguished geographer—I believe it was he—once made the true remark that there was not enough mechanical or engineering ability in all Arabia to build one battleship. Between ourselves, I should mourn the day when Arabs began to build battleships as a day of man's desolation and shame!

The solution of the problem of peace is thus twofold: To enrich the fund of shared culture and the scope of active cooperation. To cherish the kernels of separateness and regional genius with a solicitous care. It is this latter spirit which may preserve those regions, by scrupulous nonexploitation, from the pressure to compete and be not almost but altogether like ourselves. In addition to the legal approach, there must be the approach of the believer in the wisdom of God, for whom the variety of mankind is prophetic of distinctive roles in human destiny. The solution which makes for peace is never a mere work of law, and it is never merely found; it had to be made, as a work of art is made. We have to reconstruct the different within the frame of the universal, so as to give each its distinctive function. The community of the world will then more resemble an orchestra than parliamentary assembly or town meeting.

And while a work of art has its logic, it must always be a work of love.

And education for peace may well begin with the field of art, in which instinctive admiration is always combined with a recognition of unbreakable regional distinction. Then follow on with religion, where the variety of routes to the divine is as evident as the identity of the divine itself. The one tie of men which leaves all the differences free to assert themselves naturally thus rises to its full importance as an international bond, the common worship directed to the God of all men, before whose august will the competitive concerns sink to their true proportion and, while making endless problems for the future, never assume the flagrant importance of driving human brethren to mutual destruction.

STATESMANSHIP AND CHRISTIANITY

William Ernest Hocking

IN THESE United States, we profess adherence to a principle which we call the separation of church and state. To my mind, this is a valid and important principle. It does not mean that religion and politics have nothing to do with each other, but simply that they work on each other most naturally when they are not tied up in the same organization. If religion is to act on the statesman's decisions, it must do so, not through ecclesiastical authority, but by way of the statesman's conscience. And then, again, if the statesman has his views about what the church ought to do or believe, he cannot alter the creed by legislative or executive decree, but only by such influence as his church membership allows him.

Now there are many people in the world for whom the separation of politics from religion goes far deeper. Some would say they belong to different realms altogether. In September, 1938, I was in Munich and attended one Sunday a Protestant service in a large public hall. The church of this congregation had been pulled down by some Nazi demonstrators because of the outspoken opinions of its pastor. The hall was crowded; there was only standing room for people who came in late. The sermon was on the text about turning the other cheek. "A courageous man," I thought to myself, "to speak on such a theme at such a time." But I soon discovered that it took no courage at all. For what he was saying was that there are two realms: one ideal and spiritual, in which one meets enmity with love and nonresistance; the other, worldly and practical, in which one follows the rule of resentment and retaliation and betakes oneself to force, when force can overthrow the adversary. In other words, pacifism for the realm of wishes, combat for the realm of fact; or pacifism in the heart of the Christian, warfare in his behavior. Render unto Caesar the things that are Caesar's in the *worldly* context, and unto God the things that are God's in the *spiritual* context; and do not suppose that the two contexts ever intrude upon one another's domain.

Some such separation must have existed, we think, in the mind of Bismarck, who is reputed to have been a Christian in his personal capacity, and yet was convinced that "the only sound foundation for a great power is its self-interest [state egoism] and not its romantic views." As a statesman, he acted on that maxim. On such a theory, the hope that a Christian church might influence the course of foreign policy by way of the statesman's conscience must grow very dim. For the statesman's conscience would tell him that he had no right to his Christian conscience in matters of state. And he would be a bottleneck for any influences from the Christian public, since he would judge their sentiments irrelevant.

The theory that there are and must be different codes for private life and for matters of state has a far wider spread than Germany; one might say it is almost universal. Lord Acton quotes with approval a British statesman who deplores what he calls "much weak sensitivity of conscience" in dealing with public affairs. In an essay on Walpole the elder, Mr. F. S. Oliver, reviewing the general Anglo-Saxon attitude toward political morals, has to say that the real historical question about the statesman is not whether he was an honest man who used honest methods but whether he was successful in getting and keeping power and in governing. How God judges him is God's business, but history will judge him by his patriotism and his success in promoting his state.

In our own country, there is a widespread *theological* current which, without sanctioning the statesman's choice of sticking by his state and letting his conscience take the consequences, resigns itself thereto as inevitable. The church lives in a bad world, always has and always will so live. The world's business has to be carried on by worldly men, competent and realistic, in the nonrespectable sense. These men have to survive in order to be useful; there is no value, they reason, in getting yourself killed, or excluded from the party. In order to survive, they must compromise with powers which this theology is willing to call "demonic." Now the church, in turn, say these theologians, must be realistic (in a somewhat dubious sense) about the existence of such currents; it must criticise them, but it must not refuse to live in the same world with them. Nor must it be too hard on the politician who compromises. It must allow the tares and the wheat to grow along together, both in the public fields and in the lives of individual statesmen. It must exercise a slow, humane, persuasive influence, and leave to God the final winnowing.

Now if in any of these ways, we accept the deeper separation of church and state, so that the church's conscience is *irrelevant* to the decisions of the statesman, we surrender the chief hope of the church's influence. In my opinion, this pessimistic conclusion is unnecessary and illogical. It arises from a misunderstanding (1) of the problem of the statesman, and (2) of the bearing of Christianity on public problems. Let us look at both of these matters.

The Problem of the Statesman

The sharpest apparent conflict between the principles of statecraft and the ethics of Christianity comes on the point of *selfishness*. It is generally held that self-interest is and must be the guiding principle of the foreign policy of the modern state. On this principle, the statesman will break a treaty, when it is clearly to the interest of his state to do so. He will treat alliances as pure utilities, even though the word "friendship" is used; and if the advancement of his own state is served by deserting an ally, the desertion is to take place. It is not usually advantageous to refuse the payment of debts, and therefore debts are usually paid; but a partial repudiation by devaluing the unit in which payment is made may be regarded as a useful and even laudable device, regardless of its effect on other nations. Christianity, on the other hand, is bound to condemn all these practices, being

73

committed to the love of one's neighbor as the central principle for human relations.

This contrast reaches its height when the love of one's neighbor leads to definite self-sacrifice, or the risk of one's life to save the life of another. It is hard to imagine a nation deliberately adopting a course which might lead to its disappearance as an independent state, solely for the sake of the regard which it held for another political community. It seems then that the statesman must part company with the ethics of Christianity at this point.

Now, putting aside for the moment the special acts of treachery and dishonesty we have mentioned, and giving attention solely to the general principle of self-interest, I am inclined to think that there is an important difference between self-interest and selfishness, that Christianity is opposed to selfishness in individuals and probably in states also, but that it is not necessarily opposed to self-interest. Let us see how far we can go in justifying self-interest as a basis of foreign policy, giving the statesman the benefit of every doubt. It may appear that self-interest runs counter to Christianity, not because of what it includes, but because of what it excludes.

In the first place, it is obvious that pursuing the self-interest of the state is not, for the statesman himself, selfishness. For the advantage he achieves for his state does its good, not to him primarily, but to the citizens of the nation. He is their benefactor. And they will appreciate his labors in their behalf, and call them acts of patriotism, devotion, and self-

sacrifice. What higher tribute can there be for statesman or for soldier than this, that he "spent himself in
the service of his country"? What is externally self-
interest is internally altruism.

The pious aura which great states and empires
create about the efforts of their faithful servants to
"make them mightier yet" by rank, distinction,
riches, while they live, and by the internally unanimous
honor of history given after their death, to the great
agents of expansion, such as Cecil Rhodes, is not
only a powerful motive in men's minds, but has some
foundation in truth: there is an ingredient in the mixture of self-forgetful devotion to something beyond
oneself. And if there are few statesmen who dare to
face the judgment of their own people or of posterity,
if by any misadventure of their private conscience
they should take part in "liquidating an empire"
instead of building it, we cannot forget how strong
the presumption is that "honor" lies where the public
believes it to lie.

In any event, there will be no question that to look
out for the interest of one's own state, so far as that
interest does not conflict with that of other states, is
the first duty of any statesman. No one can do good
to a wider world by neglecting his own affairs, any
more than a man can do good to his neighbor by neglecting his own solvency or his health.

No Christian, then, has any ground to object to
whatever is *positive* in the self-interest basis.

We may now take another step and note that self-
interest does not exclude doing incidental benefit to

75

other states. There is always a good self-interest reason for doing good to others, when the favor is not too
costly to one's own state; namely, the reason of
prudential reciprocity. This policy, whose maxim is,
"I'll help you, and some day you'll help me," is the
moral basis of all friendship and alliance among self-
interested states; it is as near to actual benevolence
as political realism can come. It is that "enlightened
self-interest" which some moralists have thought to
be the best ground for personal ethics.

Incidental benefits to others, as a long-range policy,
build up a strong position in the world; they put the
conferring nation in the position of a creditor, as it
were, in an unwritten bargain. The policy of British
sea power during the past two centuries, and even
longer, has illustrated this point. The long-standing
pact with Portugal, for example, has long been of more
advantage to Portugal than to England, except in
possible dangers to England which it has prevented;
but its great utility now comes to light. British sea
power has been of immense advantage to the United
States, especially during the early years of the Republic. It stood between us and the Holy Alliance,
and indeed between all of the new American Republics, fashioned out of the old Spanish Empire, and
the Holy Alliance. Great Britain was not abandoning
the ground of self-interest in doing so; it was not to
her interest to allow other European powers the kind
of political foothold in this continent that would have
brought commercial monopolies with it. But Great
Britain was not acting on an *exclusive* self-interest.

76

We can see that an exclusive self-interest would have been contrary to self-interest in the long run. It would be exclusive self-interest to which Christianity would object; and this would be equally bad statesmanship. And in so far as British action has sheltered and protected the growth of this country, a "reservoir of good will" has been built up during a century and a half which more than wipes out the unfriendly passions attending the war of liberation.

For a large part, perhaps the largest part, of the period of modern diplomacy, peace has depended on finding agreements of self-interest among great powers; though the balance-of-power policy brings in another factor, that of alliance for the negative self-interest of a common enmity, which is distinctly questionable. What the Christian will do as a statesman, in view of the possibilities of a common self-interest between states, is not merely to find them and make use of them for building up a power alignment, but more than this, to *invent them*, so that unnecessary clashes of self-interest may be resolved. And this has happened more than once in the history of our own country.

We have, however, one more step to take in the direction of self-interest. It is a dangerous step. It is full of invitations to hypocrisy. Yet it is based on one trait of the human mind which is inescapable: the fact that interest and knowledge proceed from the local center outward, and that responsibility must always be in proportion to knowledge and the ability to act. We are planted in a place; our range of action

77

has a center, just as the range of our eyes has a center. Gandhi declines to become a Christian because God placed him in India, though he sings Christian hymns every Friday. So the statesman may always truly reflect that God has placed him in his own country, and that he can never know enough about any other country, or be able to act wisely enough in behalf of any other country, to make its concerns his own. He cannot in any effective sense "love his neighbor *as himself*," or rather, "care for the interest of a neighboring country as for the interest of his own country," because of this egocentric predicament of the human political mind. The result of this is that the statesman may quite honestly believe that the best way of benefiting all mankind is by *strengthening his own state,* even if that involves the disadvantage of other states.

I say this position is full of invitations to hypocrisy. We recognize it not alone as the one used by the Japanese apologists, but also by the German apologists of 1914 (Bernhardi remarked, "For we Germans of our own nature do justice to all"). The fact that the argument is used by hypocrites, however, does not prove that it may not also be used or felt by honest men. That is our present question.

Consider, for example, the immigration policies of Canada and the United States. In 1928, at the Missionary Conference at Jerusalem, a Japanese delegate made a direct plea that Canada should be urged by the Christian church to give freer entrance to Japanese. A Canadian canon replied with much dignity and firmness that the Canadians had no intention of deserting the post to which God had called them! Here, this spokesman of the church sided explicitly with the statesmen on what might be regarded an un-Christian forgetfulness of the wider neighbor's interest. He did it as the theologian sometimes does when he is in a corner, by attributing his own opinion to the will of God. But the meaning behind that dogma is one which the Japanese government has been in times past quite willing to concede—that there is good reason for regarding certain apportionments of the earth's surface, due historically to accident and conquest, as satisfactory working boundaries for *diverse types of national life*. This was the purport of the gentleman's agreement between the two nations, well-kept on both sides, until our Oriental Exclusion Act put a sting of superfluous insult into the situation. Humanity is the richer, not when these types indiscriminately mix, but when each type has plenty of historical room to show what its own mentality can accomplish. The good of the whole is then genuinely served by a limited scope of cultural undertaking.

This is as far, I believe, as self-interest, at its longest stretch, can take us without a clash with Christianity.

It would be shirking our problem to pretend that all issues between states can be resolved in terms of enlightened and cooperative self-interest at the present moment of history. There are definite clashes of interest between states: the self-interest of one state *prescribes* an injury to another, as when Poland's ac-

cess to the sea makes a breach in the continuity of
German territory, and vice versa; or as when Japan
and China cannot both exercise sovereignty in Manchuria, in which each has important stakes. Would
Christianity have anything to say about such conflicts? Or would it propose that self-interest be subordinated to the higher principle of benevolence?

The usual reply of the statesman is that such an
issue reduces to a contest of power. It is, in the
language of the state departments, a "nonjusticiable"
issue. It is a head-on either-or issue: *either* the
people of Germany have the advantage of continuity,
or else the people of Poland have their way to the sea;
it is *either* the Japanese *or* the Chinese who have the
advantages of controlling the development of Manchuria. It is one "I will" against another "I will";
and since the essence of the state is power and not
reason, the stronger "I will" must assert itself. It is
a choice being made for the future of mankind, the
advance of one type of life and the recession of another type of life. And even so wise a man as our
own Chief Justice Holmes has said that when it comes
to a clash of different ways of life, there is no solution
except by war.

Now Christianity, as I believe, has no call to pass
judgment on the particular issues. It could hardly
offer to Japan and China the absurd advice that each
should say to the other, "Dear neighbor, *you* take
the prize." On the other hand, it must most strongly
set itself against the view that there is *any* issue
among men which can only be taken out in war.

Agreeing that the principle of doing "general good" by national advancement may be honestly held by both, and that this *self-judgment of world role* cannot be handed over to any council of arbitration or international board, it remains true that there is no longer any such issue in the world which concerns two peoples alone. If the appeal is to power, it is henceforth an alignment of world forces that will be called on for the settlement. An alignment of the judgments and political intuitions of free states would be at least equally relevant to the rightness of the result. The word of Christianity to the statesman, then, is simply that he must from henceforth *abandon the principle of moral solitude* in problems affecting the status of his own nation. He is bound to strive without cessation to bring the *mind* of mankind to bear on whatever so affects the *good* of mankind as a question of peace and war. This requires that the mind of mankind be organized for that purpose, which is one reason for a new league.

Our conclusion, so far, is that the problem of the statesman certainly does not require him to put Christianity into another compartment. He must make the self-interest of his state a primary principle, but this does not mean *exclusive* self-interest. And he must insist on the state's self-judgment, its being judge in its own case regarding its role in history, but not on its *solitary* self-judgment.

And as the world moves toward becoming an actual community of nations, acknowledging a superior law to the law of the separate state, many of those personal deviations from the code of personal honor, supposed to be characteristic of diplomacy—such as lying to your rival, breaking your treaty, double-crossing your ally, international logrolling without regard to principle, compromising with the power whose aid you want to use, all the chicanery and sham of diplomatic pretense—will become as devastating to the state or statesman who indulges in them as they now are to the repute of the private citizen in his own community under law.

Statesmen have been known to cheat for the sake of their country, not because the cause of their country was indefensible, but because they were not quick-witted enough to gain the legitimate object the honest way. They could not wreck their country's case solely on the score of their own stupidity, hence they stacked the cards. Many a good man has thus lowered his own level of principle on becoming an ambassador or foreign minister. (I could give contemporary instances, but refrain from doing so. Each of you can supply his own examples.) These are problems that belong to the biography of the statesman rather than to the inherent connection of Christianity with statesmanship itself.

The issue of principle which we have reached is simply this: Enlightened self-interest of states, in the modern world, runs increasingly close to what positive benevolence would propose. But at heart it is not benevolence at all; it is self-interest. And Christianity can hardly be content with the counterfeit.

There is also a difference in actual results, if one systematically tries to see things from the other man's point of view.

This is a genuine issue. And in regard to it, we cannot prescribe that the statesman shall be a Christian. If he is not, it is useless for him to pretend, as too often he does pretend, that he is animated solely by motives of benevolence and good neighborliness; the piercing of that pretense would leave his emotional relations with his neighbor worse than if he avowed the cold truth. But the point is, that Christianity, if it were actually there in spirit, *would not wreck foreign policy;* and further, it might actually create the substance called good will. Now good will is an "intangible," and the nonrespectable realists cannot manufacture it; but it is a solid asset in business, and none the less so in diplomacy, if the *real article* can be had. I shall even venture to say that it is the *only* substance that will hold together the difficult world of the next hundred years. If Christianity can inject into statesmanship some of this precious substance, it will make the greatest and most practical contribution to the world's peace. But herewith we come to our second question: What has Christianity to say to the statesman?

What Has Christianity to Say to the Statesman?

Just as it is a false idea of statecraft to suppose that a good foreign policy is necessarily selfish, so it is a false idea of Christianity to suppose that it would dictate a foreign policy which would necessarily ruin the state.

The supposition that Christianity demands the impossible in politics is a natural impression if one takes the language of the Sermon on the Mount as a series of political injunctions. This language is with difficulty applied to the human individual; it is not strange that it applies with even more difficulty to the life of states. But what is its meaning and application?

We may accept the view that, in their spirit, the injunctions of the sermon are the kernel of Christian ethics, especially those relating to the nonresistance of evil, to taking no thought for the morrow, to the love and forgiveness of enemies. But there are two things to remember about them. First, they are devoted to making a sharp contrast between the old teaching and the new and therefore are drawn with strong light and shade. Second, they are directed to the inner disposition rather than to the outer behavior. And because they apply to the psychological interior, to the "heart," they definitely *do not apply* to beings who have no such interior. Before transferring them directly to the behavior of states, as determined by statesmen in their official capacity, we must consider whether a state, apart from the persons who compose it, has its own private heart and feelings. The difficulty of this question is made clear if we reflect on the dictum of one of the early popes (was it Innocent IV?), who, observing that the state could not be saved nor damned in another world, decided that it could not have a soul. If, however, the citizens have souls, and if the acts of the state are done in their name, the Sermon on the Mount cannot be wholly irrelevant.

Let us carry these thoughts to three topics on which the gospel has been supposed to have a direct word to statecraft—to pacifism, to punishment, and to the equality of nations.

1. *As to pacifism.* The precepts about turning the other cheek and the nonresistance of evil are set in contrast with the older principle of retaliation, an eye for an eye. The inner contrast is between anger and hate on one side and love on the other, a love directed to one's enemy. The difficulty, in personal life, is not in the nonresistance but in the love. Anybody can check the impulse of striking back; anybody can startle his enemy by adding to the cloak the coat also. But the whole point lies in the motivation of these acts.

This is why Immanuel Kant insisted that, in public life, to yield to an aggressor is always wrong. For yielding may be the act of a coward, or of one who is simply too idle to take the trouble to react. And no one will suggest that the Master was offering approval for any such poltroonery, still less commanding it. Nonresistance, if it is to have spiritual value, must be the work of a hero, not of a coward; there must be more and not less of courage in it than in the usual strike-him-back behavior. It is completely essential to the meaning of the gospel that the clearest distinction be made between the new behavior and that moral worthlessness which it outwardly resembles.

How can this distinction be made? Only by the actual and conspicuous presence of *love and thought* on the part of the nonresister. His nonresistance must be a direct assertion to the belligerent that "this is not the way to solve our difficulty"; but one who asserts this negation must be prepared with an affirmation, "This *is* the way." Otherwise his action remains a mere sentiment, as if to say, "I love you, and therefore I propose to yield everything you are fighting for." And this, as we realize, is appeasement, and not a solution. Wherever there is strife between human beings, there is a reason. Pure, meaningless aggression is the rarest of events. And therefore the Christian will look into the reasons, and with the postulate: there is a settlement which will be satisfactory to my neighbor and will leave us in amity as brethren. One who can meet a difficulty in this way is clearly the bigger man, in terms of mental and sympathetic comprehensiveness; and Christianity is a summons to greatness, not to shrinkage.

This being the meaning of the commandment, can it or can it not apply to statecraft?

The answer depends partly on (1) whether the non-resister can actually love his enemy, and (2) whether he does actually have a better solution, which is not equivalent to abandoning his own case.

As to the first point, it is doubtful whether a state, *as such,* can love its enemy. Here we meet the difficulty about the emotions of a corporate body like the state. This is not a fictitious trouble; for a state is composed of people having numerous divergent dispositions and ideas. It is not sufficient that the *statesman* be a Christian and love individual members of the other state. It must be a genuine disposition from state to state. Now there are such dispositions, in the form of dominant friendly prejudices, historic mutual aid, the multitude of internal ties of language and custom and culture, of which we have already spoken. If good will is a reality, as we have urged, so is the tradition of good will, such as the long record of settlements reached by arbitration between Britain and the United States. But these sentiments, directed to specific members of the family of nations, are just the things that fail us when we are confronted by an "enemy" nation; and it is just the enemy and not the friend that Christianity would have us love. And if an actual feeling of love is wanting it *cannot be improvised.* It is worse than useless, a falsehood which the enemy will at once detect, if the statesman pretends for the enemy's people a friendliness of spirit which is actually not there. And if it were there, it is hard to see how it could be made unmistakably visible to an enemy who had cut off intercourse by a belligerent act. Personal combat has the quality of bringing the contestants into particularly close relations, so that the language of each to the other can be heard and felt. War between states has the quality of cutting off intercourse, even of the remote diplomatic variety, and of substituting for it the arguments of the quarry and the bomb. Under such circumstances, nonresistance, even motivated by love, could not be distinguished from *yielding;* and the whole point of the gospel injunction would be lost.

87

As for the work of thought in proposing a better solution, the presumptions of warfare, whose beginning in modern times must be long prepared, require us to suppose that any such solutions would already have become known to the aggressor. He fights because already he has rejected them and proposes to have his own way, by *force majeure.* To strike back, in these circumstances, would not be a work of retaliation. It would be simply a *forcible rejection of the method of force,* in order that the opponent might once more be induced to resume human conversation. In that conversation, love and thought can resume their sway. Fighting, for the Christian, is an effort to bring the enemy within the reach of the power of love.

Pacifism in these circumstances is either a failure to do, or a deferment of doing, this preliminary labor. But let me say this for the pacifist: While states can seldom love states, individuals gifted with love *can love whole peoples.* They become the most precious members of the community when the time for resuming conversation arrives. For *they alone can heal the wounds of war.* No state would do well to violate the spirit of these men by requiring them to fight.

I conclude that an application of the meaning of the Sermon on the Mount in respect to pacifism does not forbid a resort to defensive warfare, but applies both before the aggression starts and after the war is concluded. And during the war it prescribes the humble remembrance that we are fighting because both our

love and our intelligence have fallen short of their
mission. We come to our second topic:

2. *As to punishment.* Here I shall be brief, but
none the less emphatic.

Even more than love, forgiveness is a unique element in the Christian demand. The relation of the
individual to God is hung on the pivot of forgiveness:
as we forgive so are we forgiven.

Forgiveness, like love, is a personal and creative
language. One may forgive an enemy *in absentia;* but
the forgiveness does its destined work of establishing
a new beginning only when the forgiven person can
recognize the presence of acceptance and restoration
of status and the spirit in which it is offered. Unless
he does recognize this, and is made over by it, forgiveness is simply a failure of justice, an error in the
karma of human history. He who forgives assumes
a heavy moral burden. To assume such a burden is
appropriate as between individuals; is it appropriate
as between states?

Now the central miracle of Christianity is rebirth;
and this miracle passes between man and man, and
also between God and man. Can it pass between corporate entities?

I should say that the presumptions were all against
it, if I had not known it to occur. It did occur for a
brief moment at the close of the last war. There was
an interval of a few months between the armistice and
the conclusion of the Versailles Treaty when Germany
assumed that the Fourteen Points of Wilson, together
with other engagements made in his public speeches,

would be incorporated into the treaty and that a genuine start would be made toward a new Europe. Many Germans felt that this was better than they had either hoped or deserved and went out of their way to express both repentance and a boundless zeal for the new order. I need not relate the disappointments that followed as a result of the direct violation of certain engagements of the armistice, nor undertake to judge them. All I point out here is my own conversion to a belief that forgiveness may also reconstitute the spirit of a nation.

But here again the statesman cannot, as a man, forgive the wrong which his people have suffered. It is they who must do this, though he may lead them in that direction. He can diminish their sense of self-righteousness by a sufficiently careful reading of history. He can point out that the building of a new world order must begin with a revising of our own household habits. He can do something to stem the current of revenge and destruction of the cultural life of the ex-enemy people. But he cannot pretend for them a forgiveness which they do not feel nor believe in.

The chief brakes against revenge in the modern world are simply that punishment becomes impossible as directed against a whole people. Individuals may be, and should be, brought to justice. But the punishment for making war is the war itself, and the loss of it, the long burden of ruin and regret, and the verdict of history. To attempt to add to this by humiliations, exactions, and dismemberments is not to punish the culprit nation so much as to punish the world and to leave a swamp of mental misery and disease in the heart of the era which should mark a rebirth of hope for man.

To put it simply, warmaking is a crime too great to be punished, for all the means of punishment react upon the punisher. Our dilemma is clear: we shall either stumble into the period ahead, with mounting problems and diminishing capacity to meet them, or we shall take on the outward semblance of those who, doing what justice they can, forgive the rest in order to begin anew. And the more genuine Christianity we can pour into this form, the better for the world. This is where we can use some of our pacifists.

3. *As to equality.* The equality of men in the sight of God is not, so far as I know, a doctrine of Scripture. As I read the Bible, God is active in making distinctions of a moral order, as between the sheep and the goats. But even if it were a doctrine of Scripture, this would not carry with it as a corollary the equality of *human groups* such as nations. It is hard to give this phrase any concrete meaning.

Equality before the law is a status attributed to citizens by political groups in order that the laws may be stated in perfectly general terms. In order that this attribution of equality may not run too wide of the mark, states make certain conditions for their membership: the modern state welcomes a degree of diversity in its racial composition, but not so wide a diversity that its mature members do not have a certain homogeneity of mentality and outlook.

But the equality of which our liberal founders speak, when they say that men are born equal, is the equality of natural liberty. As Locke put it, one man is equal to another in the sense that "God hath not given to any other the right to rule over him." It belongs to the definition of a man that he regulates himself by dint of his own thinking; in so far as someone else thinks for him, he ceases to be a man. When he runs out of knowledge, he asks questions, and uses the answers; he does not ask the person he questions *to take charge of him!* Every man is by definition a self-regulating organism; and in this liberty he is the equal of every other. Christianity adds to this picture two elements: God requires of him the responsible use of this liberty, and so presumes the liberty itself; God loves each one and seeks to win him to that right use of liberty which comes from a return of love to his heavenly Father. Thus the idea of equality, both in the democratic state and in Christian theology, turns around the notion of liberty as natural to man and as essential to his development as a man.

Here Christianity has, I believe, a direct requirement to make of the statesman. It demands that no political arrangement shall be set up anywhere which shall deprive men of liberty in respect to the fundamental moral choices of their lives. There must be no political order which compels their decisions in regard to livelihood, belonging, and ultimate allegiance, so far as they are prepared to think these decisions out for themselves. They must be free to make their own mistakes in order that finding the right way may be a result of their own volition. This means that no group of men may be regarded as the *political property of any other group,* or utilized by that other group for purposes in which the dependent group does not share. It does not mean that tutelage is not in order in some cases, but it means that not even tutelage can cover the whole of the life of the dependent group and that its destiny must be to give way to self-government.

It means, too, that certain basic rights of man to his mental and moral freedom must be ensured by every government, as a minimum human charter whose authority is higher than that of the laws of any land.

But this requirement does not carry with it the consequence that human groups are equal or that nations are equal or that every nation has the right of self-determination. The propensity of Christian thinkers to carry over from the right of the individual to the right of the national group brings a certain perplexity to the statesman. He is impressed by the alterability of national groupings and their great variability in size, development, power. Lichtenstein might be a province in any one of the states it touches; is it then an equal, solely because it is politically separate? Is each principality in the Indian peninsula a state and equal in some sense to the whole in which it is embedded, or perhaps superior at present, since the rest of India is still a colony?

There is an equality of another sort. The ideal of a society of nations under law, which we met with in our first hour together, must remain as a goal for which the Christian will strive. Such a society will have its membership, and as members there will be a new equality before the law of nations. But such equality does not drive out inequality. And with the faults of large nations who argue from their own greatness in one respect to their superiority in all, there goes the corresponding fault of small nations who argue from their equality before the law to their equality in weight in all international counsels. The egoism of great states is a menace to world liberty; the egoism of small states is a menace to world order and tranquillity. And since there are more small states than great ones, and each small state has more things than any large state about which to envy its neighbors, the amount of discontent which small states can generate may be said to be in inverse ratio to their size. Christianity must beware of the assumption that either the great state or the small state is always in the right. There is required an ethic of inequality to use in conjunction with any ethic of equality, and this has still to be worked out.

The greatness of Christianity is that it has a perennial guide to the simplification of the almost infinitely complex problems of international order. Without regarding the nation as an unimportant grouping, nor race as unimportant—it is vastly important—it looks through these intermediate bundlings of men to the individual human person in his relations to the God of all mankind. Not prescribing what these bundlings shall be, it sets up certain negative rules:

No men shall be property of others.

No men shall be used as mere means to the purposes of others.

No men shall be held back from any freedom which they are ready to exercise.

No one man or group of men shall be the sole judge of the destinies of any other man or group of men.

If the statesmen will but observe these conditions, the church may well set them free to mold the maps of the future world, since the spirit of Christ will then mold its inner life.

But Christianity has a more positive message to the statesman. It is suggested in Article XIX of the Covenant of the League of Nations. This article gave an important function to the Assembly of the League, that is to say, to the body on which all the member states were represented, and which therefore had the widest sweep of knowledge of conditions in the world. It authorized (and, in effect, required) the Assembly "to advise the reconsideration by Members of the League of treaties which have become inapplicable and the consideration of international conditions whose continuance might endanger the peace of the world." This we might call the watchdog function of statesmanship. It went beyond the traditional functions of dealing with troubles as they arise; it called on the statesman to concern himself with probable trouble *before it arose,* and to do so by making the problems of the neighbor state his own problems.

Now if there is any one point on which the League may be said to have failed, when it need not have failed, it was in the observance of Article XIX. The members, especially the great powers, knew where mischief was brewing. They did nothing about it, commensurate with the difficulty. They tried through private palliatives, which we now call appeasement, to deal with radical maladjustments in which explosions were being prepared. Leadership in these trouble spots passed into the hands of unscrupulous and desperate men, not so much because there were no solutions in sight as because nobody was making a serious effort to find the solution. Each power was minding its own business, while the League was calling on them all to mind the distress of the neighbor.

Now there are plenty of intrusive and busybody ways of meddling with the affairs of other nations. But when the trouble is a disease spot which, in the language of Article XIX, "might endanger the peace of the world," minding one's business becomes international *ostrichism,* if you will allow me the word. The growing interconnectedness of the world has brought it nearer to the condition of an organism, a "One World" condition, in which the welfare of each part is an integral factor in the welfare of every other part.

"Bear Ye One Another's Burdens"

Here the Christian principle spurs the statesman to the positive conception of his duty. It does not say, Mix up the world into a homogeneous brew; it does not say, Indulge in universal charity; it does not say, Give prizes to the most fecund of peoples and make more room for them the more they multiply. But it does say: Take your neighbor's troubles into grave

96

consideration, for they are also your troubles. Make the standard of living of all parts of the world a matter of your own concern. Be ready to give aid, within your power, and to invest in the invaluable substance of good will. Help to make the world a place of mutuality and brotherhood, in which the very differences among men are valued and respected. Then the Christianity you profess will take visible form over the years, and we shall know in the historic sense the new and growing meaning of the saying, "And the Word was made flesh, and dwelt among us." Those who would remove Christianity from bearing on statesmanship have lost sight of half of the meaning of the Incarnation.

THE CHURCH, THE PRESS, AND
WORLD OPINION

WILLMOTT LEWIS

THE temptation must be strong upon any man of my trade to ask whether today, any more than yesterday, the church—or the churches—or those who minister in the churches—are in fact attached to freedom of speech and information. This freedom stands for toleration, which has not always been cherished by the theologian. Less than two years ago Professor Coker of Yale remarked that in a sense it might be said that the Puritans and some others came to America to escape from a system of toleration. He turned to Nathaniel Ward (author of the Massachusetts "Body of Liberties") to support what he said. "I lived in a city," said the good Nathaniel, "where a Papist preached in one church, a Lutheran in another, a Calvinist in a third. . . . The religion of that place was but motley and meagre, their affections leopard-like." He added sternly: "He that is willing to tolerate any Religion, or discrepant way of Religion, besides his owne; . . . either doubts of his owne, or is not sincere in it." Roger Williams rebelled against this highly authoritarian system, and the day came when Cotton Mather—even he!—agreed that Williams had had "the root of the matter in him."

Now let us look for a moment at the press, the great distributor of information, the agency which (with the radio) represents that daily diffusion of consciousness to which the mind of the modern man is exposed. Look at any great newspaper, and what do you find? Its pages offer a hundred imperfect images, none of which can even be approximately realized; they make demands upon the thinking capacity of man which—it is to be feared—run beyond its growth. A witty friend of mine—now alas! dead—once said that mental culture seems to reverse the process of agriculture, passing from the intensive to the extensive, and going to seed over a wider and wider area, regardless of the fertility or infertility of the soil. And all this, remember, while there are new millions of participants in the control of general affairs who must now attempt to form personal opinions upon matters which were once left to a few.

Liberty to inquire and to print, at whatever cost to ancient beliefs and traditional disciplines—where have they for the time being left us? "What do people mean," asked the great Lord Acton, "who proclaim that liberty is the palm, and the prize, and the crown, seeing that it is an idea of which there are two hundred definitions, and that this wealth of interpretation has caused more bloodshed than anything—except theology?" I have no answer, and if any man has one, his reading has been wider than mine.

The world now at war stands, ironically enough, for an achieved growth of the human mind. Of our "many inventions" two have been beyond others important, for they have helped to create a social memory that endures beyond death. There is language, which extends enormously the field of cooperation and common action, and there is writing, which enables us to record for our posterity all that we consider worth remembering. Without these two inventions we should not have the vast and intricate structures, religious, political, social, and scientific, which dominate our lives. Yet it is with human institutions as it is with the human body—they can get clogged with the waste products of their own working, they can become the instruments of their own frustration. It is recorded of William James that he once complained to a friend that "the natural enemy of any subject is the professor thereof." Karl Marx said, a year or so before he died: "You may call me anything you like, but you must not call me a Marxist." And I ask reverently what our Lord might say if he returned to us.

You need not seek reasons for this any deeper than human nature. If you are to advance into the arena of reform, you would be wise to go softly, taking counsel from Stevenson's "Fable of the Four Reformers." When they assembled, each came with a favorite panacea of his own. One wished to abolish property, a second the Bible, a third the laws. But the fourth was impatient with these cowardly half-measures. "The first step," he said, "is to abolish mankind." I think the fable has a moral. We must use our institutions, but if we begin by pinning our entire faith upon them, we end by losing our faith in man.

There is a sense in which the duty of the church is what Finley Peter Dunne declared to be the duty of the newspaper—to comfort the afflicted, and to afflict the comfortable. We should remember the saying to-day, when economic science (so-called) seems to be adrift as we move toward a postwar world stricken with poverty, when the comfortable among us are tempted to consider their own security as the first and indispensable element of general progress, and when the question of all questions—within and be-tween nations—is whether the *remedies* for the ills from which we suffer may not be as unbearable as the ills themselves.

There are dissensions among us, but this is not a new thing. Let me borrow a story from an English scholar, who told how, once upon a time, much longer than 6,000 years ago, the trilobites—small marine organ-isms now extinct—were the only people that had eyes. They were only just beginning to use them; some even among the trilobites had as yet no signs of coming sight; and the utmost they could know was that they were living in darkness and that perhaps there was such a thing as light. But at last one of them, more advanced than his fellows, happened to come to the surface of the water in the daytime, and he saw the sun. So he went down and told the others that in general the world was light, and that one great light caused it all. Then they killed him for disturbing the commonwealth; but later they came to consider it impious to doubt that in general the world was light and that there was one great light which caused it all. And they had great disputes about the manner in which they had come to know this. Afterwards an-other of them, advanced beyond his fellows, happened to come to the surface of the water in the nighttime and saw the stars. So he went down and told his fellows that in general the world was dark, but that nevertheless there were a great number of little lights in it. Then they slew him also, for maintaining false doctrines. But from that time there was division among them, some maintaining one thing, and some the other.

When all could see, there was perhaps an end of the matter; although—looking out upon the world of our time—I doubt it. I doubt, moreover, whether we who have come after the trilobites have yet been given that sight which is clearer than bodily vision. Priests and teachers and journalists, we all serve what I hope I may without offending call agencies of mass impression; by how much does the church or the school or the newspaper deserve the charge that it offers, not a vision of reality, but an escape from reality? By how much, before the curtain rang up on the tragedy in which we are all actors, had they prepared those to whom they minister to face the brutal reality of force? I ask the question because I think it should be asked, not because I have a condemning answer. When once again resort to war as (in Clausewitz' words) "a continuation of policy" fell over the world like a shadow, how many among us had more to offer than negation and a suspension of belief? Where did the pulpits and the editorial columns of the English-speaking nations stand? Will they tomorrow set themselves against a return to the anarchy of interna-

tional relations, where hostile states reach the flower
of their development in war?

These are honest questions, and an honest answer
might help us when the time comes to make the world
over—if we can—in the image of an enduring peace.
The press can do much, and the church can do much,
but not if they do not work in a sufficient unity of purpose. What *are* the realities of this world, as the
churches see them? The layman's vision may be
limited, but he sees that they cannot be expressed
solely in terms of pieties and principles, for these can
become as heavily encrusted with parasitic growths
as a plant. When Dr. Johnson said that patriotism
could be the last refuge of the scoundrel he did not go
far enough. A constitution (written or unwritten), a
bill of rights, a Magna Carta, a pious precept, are in
the same case. There is no wiser among the wise sayings of an older time than that which tells us that the
corruption of the best becomes the worst—*corruptio
optima pessima*. Liberty can become license, and the
passion for equality can decline into envy. As for
secular knowledge, we have seen where it can lead us.
If we define "good," for instance, as all that assists
man's conquest of nature, we must define "evil" as
all that assists man's conquest of man—workaday
definitions which stand for the paradox of our life. It
is not only when war comes that this is manifest; it
is tragically true in time of peace, within nations as
between nations. There is scant comfort in a famous
saying of Francis Bacon:

Let none be alarmed at the objection of the arts and sciences being depraved to malevolent or luxurious purposes and the like, for the same can be said of every worldly good: talent, courage, strength, beauty, riches, light itself.

But there is one problem above all others—and that is war. The chemical and mechanical engineers of our day know, as the average layman cannot know, what the development of science holds in store for a world which has not the courage to set a term to conflict between nations, or cannot restrain its greed long enough to permit the machinery of prevention to be elaborated and put to work. The machinery and the forces we use to drive it are in themselves neither good nor evil, but they have increased our power to work them for good or evil to a degree that a Newton could not have foreseen.

We must take men as they are, and accept it as true that their happiness is an affair of balance and contrast. A scholar of my acquaintance once went so far as to say that the presence of danger had become a part of our peace, that a world without it might seem stale and unprofitable. The tale of the wars of any country, he declared, can never be free from the tidal ebb and flow of the emotions of common men, the magnetic influence of fears below the threshold, the assumption that anything strange or new must be hostile, that one man's gain is another's loss. It matters little when we are thinking in terms of masses of men that the causes for which these masses will make ready and continual sacrifice are often directed against a complex of facts, geographical, historical, economic, which must in the end assert their weight. It seems that we cannot reach the underground source, the common reservoir from which the streams of action are fed. We must assume the willingness of men to set the satisfaction of a lust for power, the desire of aggrandizement, before their ease and comfort, before the accumulation of wealth, as well as before the subtler, nobler conquests which civilization holds out to the modern world. The churches surely have this bitter knowledge, for Christianity is based on knowledge of the human heart, on the doctoring of the ailments of the soul which knowledge of the heart has revealed to it.

The secular world seems, and has long seemed, to be concerned almost exclusively with its inquiry into the conditions and constitution of the material environment. The press, now become an industry devoted to the manufacture of newsprint, shares this preoccupation; it has even thrown up its millionaires. It has grown to be, as Graham Wallas said, "the most insoluble problem of democracy." Why? Because, said he, as long as his newspapers pay, and the telephone from his house to the editorial office is in working order, the owner of a group of papers has more absolute irresponsibility in the use of great power than any living man. (He wrote before the coming of the dictators.) If, said Wallas, he is to use his power in a way helpful to the community, he must aim at two virtues, veracity and seriousness; that is to say, the more obvious virtue of saying what he believes to be true, and the less obvious virtue of taking trouble to make sure that his belief is well founded. But nothing, he goes on, in his position or in the qualities necessary to reach that position, encourages either of these virtues; and the anonymous writers whom he hires to carry out his orders have neither the personal independence of artists nor the public responsibility of experts.

We all know this, with whatever honorable exceptions, to be true. And we must not forget that the prodigious growth of the press has given it a sweep and continuity of influence less only than that of government itself. The newspaper is "affected with a public interest" to a degree greater even than a common carrier, for it does not transport the bodies or the goods of men, it plays ceaselessly on the minds of men. I speak of all the English-speaking peoples when I say that the danger which confronts what we call freedom of the press is not chiefly from without— or is no longer so, now that we know our enemies will be defeated—but from within. It is, as I see it, a danger that enlarges with the increasing integration of the newspaper system—the danger that the freedom that makes the press great and useful may make some among its leaders too great, that some individuals may acquire a power which (if the freedom we demand is to be ours) they cannot be prevented from harnessing in the service of personal ambition rather than of the community from which they draw their strength. The press is one of the guardians of freedom; but, "Who shall guard the guards themselves?'' asked the stern old Roman. I have said what I have said, knowing that the same questionings fill the minds of other men of my own occupation, which is that of writer and not of publisher.

All this perhaps leads nowhere, or only to one point —that man may be smaller than his aspirations, but should not be allowed to forget them. He should be content to stop somewhere outside Utopia, and indeed will be forced to. When I was more than forty years younger than I now am, I read some words uttered by an Englishman named William Morris, and they have never left my memory. What other blessings are there in life, he asked, than hopeful work and fearless rest? What more should a man ask than to be permitted to work with hope in his heart, and to lay his head upon his pillow at night without fear? There can be but one answer to that question. And Morris said: To have space and freedom to gain these blessings is the end of politics; to learn how best to gain them is the end of education; and to learn their innermost meaning is the end of religion. There is nothing difficult, nothing recondite, in these sayings; what is important is to catch and hold their implications. I commend them to the politician, to the teacher (and the journalist is in some sort a teacher) and to the churchman.

TOWARD PEACE IN THE ORIENT

Miner Searle Bates

AS A people who wished to be let alone in order that we might fumble along with internal problems beyond our powers of mind and character to solve, we have been rudely awakened to knowledge of other continents than our own. Little conscious of the *world* of which we are a part, and of the wealth and culture and crimes in which we share, we are forcibly plunged into war. For this tragedy we of 1944 rightfully confess some measure of guilt, through ignorant and selfish sins of omission, stupid and selfish sins of commission.

The greater fault, it seems, was that of our elders and our fathers thirty years ago (1914), when in the pursuit of money and of local interests they were unprepared for their responsibilities in a world become one, yet without law and order, and twenty-five years ago (1919), when in partisan politics, tribal mind, and lack of faith, they refused even to make the experiment of constructive cooperation for peace and mutual well-being. Twenty years ago (1924), one instance among many when shortsighted self-interest overcame regard for greater relationships, we reasserted in peculiarly offensive manner our contempt for more than half the family of God. A still greater burden of responsibility, it appears to us, is upon the elders and fathers of other peoples, on both sides of the battle lines; most clearly upon the present chieftains of aggressive might and evil who led the attacks upon China, Poland, and a score of other lands, seeking to subject the earth to lust of power and pride of race. Mark the terms, "lust of power and pride of race." You will meet them again in that form and in other forms.

These attacks must be thrown back, in order that many a peaceful culture may have a chance for air and life; in order that fifteen hundreds of millions of men, immediately conquered or threatened, may have a chance to live in the moral freedom of their own institutions, with acceptable leaders of their own kind; in order that the dream of one gang looting and dominating the world may be demonstrated a nightmare and not an opportunity henceforward open to the bold; in order that mankind may have yet another chance to realize the great desire of the prophets and the sages, becoming conscious of its family character and gradually turning to organize itself for mutual well-being and the security necessary to well-being, rather than for greed, dominion, and therefore strife.

Without combined triumph of the great majority of the human race over those who would enslave them, human eye can see but ruin and despair. In winning that triumph, men will have shown such qualities of faith, courage, cooperation, and organization for a common purpose that part of the fearful injuries of war will be offset. But we shall have gained only the chance for a better era, not its guarantee. We did not use well the opportunities brought by victory in 1918. We did not use well the opportunities of peace in the years before 1914, or in the years from 1919 to the

colossal struggle of 1937-39-41. Victory and peace are
again before us, the Day of Judgment for small minds
and narrow hearts.

Victory will have been gained by overwhelming
force—not by wealth and machines alone, thank the
Lord. For vision, devotion, sacrifice, mutual trust, the
common concern of mankind, are required to assemble
and to use (beginning from circumstances highly unfavorable and of the gangsters' own choosing) the human and the material strength now marshaled. But
much of the experience of the war, to the conquered
on either side, to the victors, to the refugees, to the
prisoners, is murderous, debilitating, disorganizing to
the natural life, to the moral life, of individuals and of
societies. Grim is the destiny that requires men in
such evil case to make decisions of tremendous moment
to peace, to liberty, to welfare in the highest sense.

The stand of the Christian has always been foreshadowed in the basic attitudes required of us by the
Scriptures and most of all by our Master. Never was
this stand more needed than today. But too often the
Christian position has remained an inner longing,
vague and unrelated to the acts that make peace and
make war. The Christian outlook has been expressed
in the language of sermons, not that of generals and
admirals, nor that of diplomats and senators; still less
in the lingo of the political bosses who make senators,
and whom you and I support by indifference to how
candidates are selected and by the straight voting of
crooked tickets; seldom indeed in the language of the

National Association of Manufacturers, the labor unions, and the farm bloc.

Can the Christian love for the whole family of God, concern for the well-being of man in every race and nation, have anything to do with armistice terms; with transactions for rubber, tin and oil; with the jockeying of tariffs by our chosen representatives, most of them church members, in the Congress of the United States? If not, religion is barred from much of life, to the peril of both—barred from decisions that affect the opportunities and welfare, physical, social and spiritual, of all but hermit men.

What is the meaning, in the international relations of this century, of "Love thy neighbor as thyself"? The specific challenge of this one hour today is to bring Christian attitudes and principles squarely against the harsh realities, the stark needs, of the Orient. Are sound judgment and wise foresight in public affairs something in contradiction to Christian truth? We must on the one hand rule out the national egoist, the vengeful brute; and on the other, the blind utopian, the Cain who withdraws from the world in asceticism or perfectionism, even if labeled "Christian." Are there real possibilities of peace in the East, lines of adjustment which can express the Christian spirit and be convincing to statesmen who have to direct the social forces actually at work, and have to take the consequences of their decisions—as church conferences do not?

Through years of professional study and of varied contacts in peace and in war, I have worked upon this problem with friends of various nationalities in China and Japan, and now in this country upon the present phase, with informal but persistent consultations. What I present is an extract from that composite experience, for which I must take individual responsibility in selection and statement.

Peace must be made in political and economic, even in military terms. But those terms cannot succeed if they are merely the assertion of one national interest against another, if they are expediencies of profit and of power. Respect for the personalities of men in other national groups, concern for their opportunities as well as for our own, recognition of the fact that their destinies and ours are now and forever interlocked in one society—these attitudes are necessities of practical politics and economics; they are Christian principles at work in international relations.

Peace must take account of men as they are and as they may be, seeing squarely both the evil and the good, with an eye also to the innocence and the possibilities of children. The dreamer who thinks that a few pious words from pulpits will bring justice and opportunity for all, that the surrender of all human society to Hitler and to Tojo would have saved the world, is little more a Christian than a statesman. The one who opposes all earthly police measures because in heaven they may not be necessary, is the delight of the violent, not the shield of the defenseless. Contrariwise, the cynic who would solve all major problems by crude force is usually assuming that the preponderance of power is and will remain with his

112

gang and his views; and he is not prepared to submit those views to the prophetic judgment of a universal ethic, whether his aim is to keep his people well above all other races, or simply to smash the labor unions and farm prices in his own interests.

But why all these considerations of a general character, when the topic is the Orient? Because a primary issue is our tendency to think of the Japanese (and to some extent of other Orientals) as outside our own society and its standards, to be dealt with on a different plane. It is the old heresy and sin of putting the Samaritan beyond the range of neighborhood, the refusal to recognize even in 1944 that there is one world, that mankind is of one blood, one stock, under God.

All these fundamental considerations apply to peace in the Orient. There is not one ethic for America, another for Europe, a third for Asia. There cannot be one peace for the Americas, or one for the Western World, founded upon cooperation, and another peace for the Orient, founded upon uneasy might. What we consider to be distance, and the extent of our ignorance, do not abrogate the laws of nature and of God upon another part of this globe, this pinhead in the immeasurable universe. With all sensible regard for the particularities of those differing societies which inhabit the Orient, and those differing societies which intervene in the Orient, let our attitudes and our acts conform to reality: there is one world, under God, one human family, one human nature.

If there is one conviction to remain with us upon our subject, let it be this: There can be no peace for the world unless the Orient is at peace with itself and with the other major regions. There can be no peace in the Orient unless the rest of the world is at peace, and is in right relations with the Orient. For the Oriental peoples are half of all the peoples of the world, bound closely to the other half of us by raw materials and markets, by modern communications and information, by culture and ideas, by the very struggle for power or for peace.

Now what can be done toward a true peace settlement in the Orient?

Simple measures have been proposed. Beat the Japanese thoroughly, proceeding to give their cities full experience of destruction even after surrender has been proffered. Gain security by slaughtering most of the Japanese, or at least their leaders by whole classes; depose and chain the Emperor; destroy their system of government; wipe out what remains of their heavy industry after bombing; disarm the Japanese completely and police them for fifty years while re-educating them on lines of Western liberalism, with plenty of foreign teachers; hold as permanent American or Allied bases and garrison points the mandated islands and key positions in Japan proper; restore as rightful rulers the governments Japan has successively displaced in various lands of the Orient.

It is difficult to maintain a Christian purpose and outlook while entangled in warfare, even though the warfare be reluctant and with a constructive purpose.

But the program just described, which, with variations, you can find in many papers and speeches, is frank abandonment of respect for other personalities and concern for their opportunities, bald rejection of Christian faith in the oneness of mankind. Moreover, by its vindictiveness and one-sided character it refuses to face many of the major problems of peace in the Orient. If Americans, Chinese, and their Allies did such things, they would have brutalized themselves; they would have lost all confidence in each other's characters and motives; they would have made impossible a peaceful cooperation for reconstruction in the Orient; they would have destroyed prime factors of production in a vast population of poverty from India to Kamchatka; they would have set up a reverse imperialism of armed domination over the Japanese; they would have driven to violence and to perversion every healthy desire of the Japanese nation; they would have established in the Far East a pervasive, unstable militarism that would be the real educator of half the peoples of the earth. Who dares to say that such a course is common sense, is hardheaded practicality? The slogans of "security," "realism," "finishing the job," are often made cover for new models, American or United Nations style, of the very demons against which we are forced today to defend the higher interests of mankind.

Equally absurd is the simple program of accepting the first Japanese suggestions of a compromise peace (which would be at the cost of those weaker than ourselves and weaker than the Japanese), and its counterpart of dropping the whole matter as soon as a bare military success has been gained. That is the isolationist guarantee of another war, and soon.

The underlying problems of the Orient are these. Vast populations live for the most part in farm and village poverty, with inadequate land, inadequate methods of farming, inadequate industry and transport, to make their agricultural life satisfactory. In the tremendous sweep from the Indian Ocean to the Bering Straits, only one system of industrial and military power has been built to eminence, that of Japan, schooled by proud tradition and abnormal discipline to displace and overcome all possible challenge to its expanding rule. That unbalance of societies is basic to present insecurity.

Then there is Western imperialism, wealthy and domineering, galling to every Oriental who confronts its power and its manners. The imperial sweep is again from India, across Malaya and the islands, up the entire eastern slopes of Asia to the Arctic; and so it has been through four hundred years. Every Oriental people has felt the disturbance, the arrogance, the greed, the determining power, the economic and the military conflicts, of Western forces, which might bring knowledge, attractive goods and interests, but always by the outside will, always when and as the foreigners wished. Japan has reacted violently, and up to this moment with spectacular success, against us, the race-proud intruders. Since yesterday China has found national independence. In form, in part, or in prospect, also Thailand, the Philippines, Burma,

116

and India—to the stirring of envious self-consciousness in Indo-China, the East Indies, and Malaya. But this revival is far from complete and is still shackled by the more or less benevolent controls of Great Britain, the Netherlands, France, Portugal, and the United States. Eastern Russia remains as the immense arm of a great land power, the only domain of Western white population in permanent juxtaposition to the Orientals.

All the leaders of the Oriental peoples have gained their education and experience in years of domination of the scene by an alien race seeking wealth and power for interests not of the Orient. That imperialism has begun, for varying motives, to reform itself or even to end itself in stages. And in recent years it has been shockingly discomfited by the instantaneous counter-conquest and counterdomination of the Japanese. How shall a compromised and somewhat chastened imperialism be liquidated with the most good and the least harm to the Eastern peoples and to world-wide interests of peace and prosperity? Will the merging states of the Orientals be formed in a world of insecurity, of militarized nationalism, and economic warfare, and set their traditions accordingly? Must they fight their way, as did Japan, against social arrogance and entrenched imperial or economic privilege? Or will they find a fair opportunity in a cooperative world, with peoples considerate of mutual welfare and attempting to use the resources of God's earth for the good of all his children, instead of to seize or to hold an undue share for this nation and for that?

117

The Oriental peoples come late and ill-prepared upon the stage of modern economic life. Western lands, the United States at their head, have in hand vast accumulations of machines and technical skill, of credits and organization, pressing in desperate competition to grasp raw materials, markets, and investment profit from those who have not. Is there sufficient wisdom and self-restraint among those who direct masses of wealth and power to know the difference between exploitation and honest development, between today's profit and the prosperity of a whole generation? Throughout the Orient the common man, first in the town and gradually in the country, is coming to know the effectiveness, the economy, the convenience, the satisfactions, of modern industrial goods, tools, clothing, transportation, education, amusements. His needs, and now his conscious wants, outrun the meeting of them. The very process of modernization means heavier taxes and increased economic profits in order to develop needed mines, factories, railroads, and all the rest—to say nothing of armies and wars. The farmer and the wage laborer, who comprise nine-tenths of the population, gain dubiously and insecurely, if at all. Thus the conditions for discontent abound, discontent which may well wreck any government, and most quickly a government which permits free speech and free organization to its people.

Active, visible economic and social betterment is urgently required. If it does not come promptly by traditionally democratic methods, it will come by Japanese, German, or Russian methods. And it must come for masses of men, not for a few favored capitalists and merchants. Peace in the Orient means something far greater than destroying a Japanese city, necessary though the defeat of Japan may be. Indeed, it requires the very opposite of destruction.

The major tasks in securing peace in the Orient are seven, now to be briefly sketched.

1. *Restoration to rightful relationships and authority, with needed changes as required, of peoples and territories seized by the Japanese military.* The occupations since the invasion of China in 1937 and since Pearl Harbor are such recent and crass aggression that even Americans can remember them. Of the older conquests, Manchuria and Formosa are inhabited 95 per cent by Chinese, many of them retaining not merely cultural and economic ties with their free brethren but actual family relationships. Presumably South Sakhalin, an economic tool with few persons dwelling there, will be returned to Russia. Problems of arrangements arise chiefly in two quarters. The Koreans have made their adaptations to the modern world almost entirely under Japanese direction and will find it hard to bring forth suddenly men of such experience that they can take full responsibility for serious economic changes and for political and administrative reorganization. International assistance and supervision will probably be required for a period of years, under definite commitment to independence. The mandated islands, of strategic importance and but few people, should be held internationally as naval and air bases. They provide one of the simplest prac-

tical and psychological measures of "security" without the harmful possibilities of many other proposals. The suggestion that the islands be taken by the United States is contrary to the pledge of the Atlantic Charter and to the whole principle and spirit of cooperative undertakings for peace. Moreover, it would appear not merely to Japanese but also to other Orientals as a resumption of American nationalistic expansion in the Far East and would militate against improvements in the colonial situation in Southeast Asia.

Now these territorial changes, the important ones liberative in character, seem necessary in the interests of justice and peace alike. In no case does the Japanese claim appear so strong as other claims. The results, so far as security is concerned, will be to weaken Japan critically, throwing her back to the boundaries of 1894 and detaching important resources and industrial plans which she has developed in Manchuria, Korea, and Formosa. Geographical disarmament, that is, the transfer of significant military positions from the control of Japan to the control of those whom she has conquered or invaded, will have been achieved by other intent.

Here lie two important corollaries, the one short time, the other long in view. The transfers of territory should be clean and clear, not leaving endless grounds of dispute over the public and semipublic properties so prominent in Japanese imperialism and exploitation. If all Japanese claims and interests in the transferred territories are wiped out, and the Japanese Government left responsible for any compensation to Japanese nationals for their losses, then the slate can well be left clean on the other side. No indemnities or reparations would be saddled upon Japan, though the moral right to them may be properly asserted, and the just calculation of the fearful damage done by Japan to her neighbors might have some ideological value. Despite the complexity of this problem, and in part because of its complexity, there is great advantage for future relationships if postwar claims and compulsory collections can be removed from the prospect. Japan's impoverishment will be drastic. The impoverishment of her victims will have some assuagement in the restoration of important resources and in such fragments of plants as may remain with them at the close of the war. As a deterrent to systematic destruction, the United Nations might soon announce to Japan a program of no indemnities, qualified by replacement of any economic properties thereafter deliberately destroyed or removed by the Japanese from lands outside the home islands.

2. *Dealing with Japan in a manner conducive to lasting peace for the Orient and for the entire world.* The only sane aim is to further the development of Japan into a self-controlled and usefully participating member of the society of nations, contributing economic effort, technical skills, and cultural accomplishment to the total well-being of mankind, in which the Japanese people are a significant part. Such military occupation as may prove necessary to break the power of present leadership and to secure requisite order

should be held to the minimum in extent and in time, looking always to the constructive furthering of an independent government, wholesome for domestic and for international adjustment. Administration by outsiders and the foreign maintenance of a puppet regime are dubious anywhere, and in Japan would be peculiarly destined to ineffectiveness and disaster. Under neither program would the better type of Japanese leadership be able to make any showing, while the military assassins and ultra-patriotic cults would flourish.

With all alertness in suggestion and negotiation, the victorious United Nations should basically strive to create conditions favorable to a moderate government committed to internal welfare and unfavorable to a militaristic government bent on revenge. Relief and economic opportunity should be supplied to and through any Japanese leadership which appeared to command internal support and at the same time willing to proceed in workable relations internationally. Extension of economic opportunity in materials and trade would be understood to depend upon and to keep pace with clear demonstration that a government set toward internal development was definitely in being. The demonstration would be primarily in acts and appointments, but also in the government's statements to its own people and in its reform of constitution and procedure.

For this whole process of encouraging healthy change within Japan, the institution of the Imperial House would be a useful, perhaps the indispensable, pivot. It is impossible to imagine any other source of authority for a new group of moderate leaders determined to govern without the military chiefs. The constitutional and liberal progress which Japan made from 1867 to 1930 was made in the name of the Emperor, and the existing framework can be amended only in his name. The alternative is stark revolution, with the prizes to the most violent and the outcome otherwise unknown.

But will it not be dangerous to let the Japanese manage their own affairs? Aside from all questions of principle, aside from the administrative impossibility of doing anything else, aside from the pull of foreign soldiers to their homes as soon as the fighting is over, it should be remembered that the events of the war will in themselves bring to Japan the loss of her military equipment and of the bases which she has employed against others. Much if not all her shipping will be gone; great parts of her industrial plant will have been ceded to her neighbors or destroyed. By contrast, the United Nations generally will be in possession of the most powerful armaments in history and will hold bases ringing Japan on every side. They will also control to a large extent the economic and industrial possibilities of Japan through possession of the raw materials and markets of the Far East and of all the world. Relative to Japan, adjacent Russia and China will be much stronger than before the war. Japan could not be a menace for many a year, and will never be so, provided the United Nations evolve into a working world order.

123

3. *There must be an adequate program for the teeming peoples and rich pockets of resources in Southeast Asia.* Three childlike solutions must at once be discarded: (*a*) Use the formula of liberation from Japanese rule simply to re-establish the former regimes of colonialism and economic imperialism. (*b*) Declare the immediate independence of all groups in that complex area, most of whom are sadly underdeveloped and do not possess the educational, economic, and administrative competence or experience to set up for themselves. (*c*) Declare for international government of the entire area, when it is not yet known whether the leading countries will agree upon even a minimum program of cooperation in general affairs, and when the world's actual experience in international government is so meager and discouraging. (It might be said in passing that the international formula could be used to cloak a collective imperialism intended to outlast national imperialisms in political and economic control of undeveloped regions.)

The situations are varied. Thailand was already free, and after adjustments due to her unfortunate and considerably reluctant association with Japan, should resume her status. The Philippines and Burma, which in pledge and in fact were near to independence before the war, should, with reasonable aid and safeguards, be carried forward shortly to the determined goals. The Netherlands East Indies and British Malaya, both creditably governed and lacking the basis for present independence, should revert to the former direction, with further commitment, already foreshadowed, to more rapid political evolution. But there should be a clear measure of responsibility, logically applicable also to Burma and the Philippines, in so far as Great Britain and the United States have dominant voices in those lands, to an international authority. Asiatic personnel should be increasingly prominent in administration. The case for such interest is even stronger in Indo-China, which was managed so narrowly from Paris. Morever, there are many common problems of economic life, of migration, of culture, which call for collaboration of the various authorities in Southeast Asia, and for consideration of the region as a whole, even though the political destiny of several portions be individualized for some time to come.

4. *Peace in the Orient requires international organization on a world scale, with regional organization subordinate and supplementary thereto.* Constructive pooling of armaments for general security, provision for peaceful change and orderly settlement of disputes, the mandate principle in improved forms for areas under rival claims or not now able to maintain independence, furtherance of international trade and improvement of living standards in undeveloped regions, cooperation in the helpful exchange of information and cultural services, safeguarding of civil liberties and minority rights—all these needs of international society require world-wide collaboration, and can be met only to a limited degree by regional organizations operating separately. Moreover, so much of the whole world is actually operative in the Orient that local groupings would touch the big problems only in part.

At the same time, there are need and place in the Orient for specific agreements and continuing collaboration among the interested parties for the purposes of security and welfare already mentioned, in the regional aspects of those purposes. Obviously and rightly, such regional cooperation would tend to give greater weight to Oriental interests and Oriental leaders than entire dependence upon a global organization centered in Europe.

5. *The Orient requires for peace a world of economic opportunity with reasonable assurance of stability.* Most of its peoples are only on the threshold of modern industry, though part of them have important mineral resources. They need machinery and techniques at such a rate and in such relationships as will not increase their present disadvantages under the economic interests of wealthy giants in other parts of the world.

The Japanese, on the other hand, will be seventy millions on small and rocky islands, with economic problems more insistent than those before the war. Deprived of their exploiting hold in Manchuria, Korea, and Formosa, from which they drew much food and minerals, they will imperatively require a chance to use their technical skills in manufacture and foreign trade. The Orient needs those skills and the cheap cloth, household articles, and tools which they have supplied. Highly intensive agriculture and fishing will remain the core of Japanese subsistence; there will be great relief in the removal of the colossal burden of war preparations and also in any remedy of the feudal economic system which grinds tenant farmers and wage laborers for the benefit of concentrated wealth.

But if a fair part of these gains is secured, it is still necessary that soon and steadily Japan should again have a stable chance to get the raw materials she cannot produce from her own islands and to sell her goods abroad in order to pay for the materials and a part of her food. The alternative is misery, despair, violence, revenge. Will your congressman vote to exclude Japanese goods, and do you care? That is the test of your sincerity about peace in the Orient, which is one and the same as peace for the United States. Moreover, no government in Japan can succeed with a policy of peace unless it is promptly and convincingly assured that trade opportunities will permit Japan to live.

6. *Social and cultural advance is needful, if there is to be peace in and with the Orient.* There is not at this time occasion for hysteria about a coming world war of the races, which could mean only one line-up, whites against all others. But there is urgence in the proper human demand of all peoples that the opportunities of life for individuals and groups, including the spiritual opportunity for dignity of person and self-respect, should not be denied or abridged for the superficial reason of color. All the original, and practically all the actual, inhabitants of the Orient are members of colored races. If the world is to be run by whites on the basis of discrimination, the colored Orient cannot remain at peace with us. Moreover, if discrimination is to be the principle, the colored Orient can apply that principle in just one way—against

whites. These are the practical results of transgressing the Christian teaching and spirit. God must love the peoples of color, for he and his world have made and maintained so many of them. We can find no warrant within Christianity for arrogant and discriminatory domination of the world by the white minority, nor shall we find such warrant in any sensible social outlook upon world order.

Again, we live in one world. It is not possible for us to maintain a double-faced policy of cooperating with colored favorites abroad, such as the Chinese, and of treating at home colored peoples of any type as second-class citizens or residents. The colored peoples of the world have been taught by long and severe experience to be acutely sensitive to all discrimination. For example, Chinese are mildly appreciative of our recent removal of the long-standing stigma put upon them by our naturalization and immigration laws. But they have a twofold reason to think that this is merely an expedient of war to encourage a needed ally, without breaching our fundamental attitude toward all peoples of color, including themselves. For they observe the discriminations habitually borne by our Negro fellow citizens, and they see clearly that all other Orientals still remain under the old bans. Nothing short of complete justice and friendliness can meet the issue of race and give the world a chance to face the universal problems of spirit and of organization without that wretched, unnecessary complication. This has tremendous significance for the peace in the Orient.

Europe and America are linked, not merely by manifold ties of blood, but also by ties of history and culture. Much less close are the actual ties, and the consciousness of those ties, between the Orient and the Western World. Linguistic relationships are distant and difficult. These facts bring the greater need for mutual contact in culture and education. We have much to learn about each other and from each other. At present they and we alike are too easily prey to the indifference, the social hostility, the uncritical prejudices, which are due as much to ignorance as to lack of sympathy. Our minds and hearts are 400 years behind Columbus and Magellan, because many of our schools and churches do not yet act upon the knowledge that the earth is round. This is a field of effort for peace peculiarly suited to the churches, with their interests and resources in the missionary relationships. The field ought to be entered with ten times the boldness, vigor, and comprehensiveness that we have ever seen.

7. *There are tremendous matters which we may call margins and methods, too easily passed by in the selection of a few great issues for brief treatment out of the whole problem of peace in the Orient.* It is customary to leave out Russia from such considerations, because she has for some fifteen years been relatively inactive in the Orient, and because she is not today fighting in that area. India also is frequently omitted, whether by geographical definition or because her problem is distinctive and enormously complex in itself; but in any case, like Russia, Australia, and New

Zealand, she is in some measure upon the fringes, and has had major relationships elsewhere. Moreover, India has not been the scene of war, nor have her people thus far taken a part in the war proportionate to their numbers and resources. The later years of the war are likely to see both Russia and India as more active participants in the Orient, and certainly the making of peace and the long-time relationships involve both lands as important factors.

Here India can be mentioned only as the most conspicuous and influential test in the whole issue of Western imperialism in the Orient. Now as never before, it is true that no nation liveth unto itself alone, and the basic attitudes of England, India, China, the United States, Japan, and many other lands are tied up significantly in the fate of India. Some Americans are reckless in their orders to the British Empire, shouting them forth with an ignorance, tactlessness, and refusal to examine our own shortcomings which are thoroughly unhelpful. We must remember that we have heartily built up our economic interests in India and the whole of Eastern Asia upon the advantages secured by British, Dutch, and other imperial systems. We have usually escaped the responsibility and much of the criticism; we have secured the desired benefits under "favored nation" clauses, under the benevolent policies of the open door and of equality of opportunity. Moreover, we have shown no sign at any time of submitting to international check and correction our economic absorption of the Philippines or our miserable record in Puerto Rico. Advance in India is needed on many grounds, not the least of which is as a move toward peace in the Orient. It is most likely to be achieved by the Indian and British peoples themselves, in an atmosphere of all-round devotion to liberal, cooperative progress for the sake of world-wide peace and welfare. The equivalent tests for the United States will be rubber, tin, oil, and gold, in their bearings upon peace and constructive development in the Orient and throughout the world.

But India and Russia, still more China and other lands and interests of the Orient proper, raise a further question of method—acutely important to peace. We Americans, idealists as well as those who claim the name of realists, are inclined to set our minds very definitely upon what must be done to secure peace, the kind of peace we want or the kind of peace which our minds are conditioned to think out. We need a thousand times to remind ourselves that we have a great responsibility for our part in the whole matter of the war and the peace. But it is only a part. The central elements in the Orient are the people who dwell in the Orient, who *are* the Orient. Even among outsiders, others have been more important than we, and may still be so in the future. The war itself is a global enterprise, in which no man will ever be able to weigh justly the contributions of China, of Russia, of the British peoples, of ourselves, to say nothing of others.

The making of peace and the keeping of peace require genuine adjustment and cooperation among the United Nations, also with neutrals, and with our present enemies. To attempt to determine the pattern in

America, and then in the name of righteousness to use our military and economic power to force the world into that pattern is colossal hypocrisy and colossal imperialism—doomed from the outset to terrible failure.

Adjustment and cooperation are not one-way jobs under American management. The man who is always asking, "But will the Russians play the game?" "Can we trust the Chinese to stay with us?" betrays his localism. For the rest of the world is asking, with poignant memory, whether the United States will play the game, whether the richest and most powerful member of the world community will act as a democratic, dependable neighbor. Do we have the character and the intelligence to use our fearful power in honest organization with others to meet the problems of the whole community? Peace for the Orient, now and through coming generations (therefore, peace for us, for our descendants, and for the world), depends in great measure upon the answer of our deeds.

In stern, beneficent judgment, God observes us this day and throughout these fateful years. To us much has been given, and from us much will be required. He does not watch us through lenses made in America, nor through lenses that are white. For he will judge with equity all the peoples of the earth.

A CHRISTIAN VIEW OF INTER-AMERICAN RELATIONSHIPS

GONZALO BAEZ-CAMARGO

WHEN Sir Norman Angell, in his book, *Let the People Know,* arrives at the conclusion that the fundamental reason for this war is the nationalistic isolation that refused to admit the spirit and set up the system for international cooperation and security, he not only strikes at the bottom of all conflicts between nations but also brings forcefully forward, without calling it such, a Christian view of international relationships. Because the essential message of Christianity through the centuries regarding human relations, among individuals as well as among groups or nations, is cooperation and mutual help.

If it has taken twenty centuries for men to begin to realize that this truth must also be applied to international relationships, the blame is not on the Christian gospel, but on those who, in leading positions, have taken no heed to it, perhaps because they thought that it had to do only with private individual living and not with collective behavior as well. The blame is undoubtedly shared by us, the majority of Christians whose witness and action have not been effective enough to impress that truth on the leaders of the nations. Thus the Machiavellian doctrine that states must each be and have their own law and enforce it by sheer economic or military power has had its own way and thrown mankind periodically into the infernal cauldron of war, each time more destructive and more nearly universal than before.

It is a good sign indeed that an increasing number of the best minds in our times are turning, consciously or unconsciously, to the Christian way. The whole trend in international thinking is now away from national egotism and isolation, and in the direction of good will, friendship, and closer cooperation. The traditional view of absolute national sovereignty and independence—the "me for myself alone" theory—is in the grip of a death crisis. Its thorough revision is being pressed by the brutal experience of war. It would have been enough, in order to discover its weakness, to bring it courageously under the floodlight of the gospel.

We of the Americas, being relatively far removed from the immediate scenes of the war, are in a better position than the rest of the world to give straight thought to the problems in international relationships. The end of Machiavellianism, as M. Maritain, the French philosopher, has recently proved, is almost certain. We have a splendid opportunity of helping to shape the international doctrine that must replace it. Furthermore, we have the unique chance to begin to demonstrate that doctrine in our own relationships. This is why a Christian view of inter-American relationships becomes so important. Let us try to outline it. But first let us consider our background.

The Birth of the Americas

The most important date in the history of the world, with the single exception of the day our Lord Jesus was born, is October 12, 1492, the day when Columbus discovered the New World. That discovery not only brought about a tremendous economic, political, and social revolution in Europe, but it also gave birth to nations destined to play a large role in the affairs of the world. This continent was called America, after its first cartographer. It should have been called Colombia, after the discoverer. There is some confusion in the present use of the name "America." You in the United States of America use it, by shortening your official name, for your country, while we of the southern republics still love to use it in its larger meaning for the whole continent. In the present paper, only in order to avoid the confusion, I shall in referring to the continent use the plural, "the Americas."

Geographically, there are three Americas commonly mentioned. Actually, there are four: North America, Central America, South America, and the Caribbean Islands or West Indies, which might be called Antilian America. Racially and culturally, there are at least six Americas: the original Indian America, distributed throughout the continent, with its heaviest populations in Mexico; Central America (excepting Costa Rica); South America (with the exception of Argentina and Uruguay); then, Anglo-Saxon America, that is, Canada and the United States in their main racial structure; Spanish America, all the way down from New Mexico and California to Argentina and Chile (except Brazil, where we find Portuguese America); there is also an African America, with its population distributed between Haiti, Cuba, the United States, and Brazil mainly; finally, there is what we may call a general European America, in which certain areas, where European immigration has not been assimilated, are to be included. For instance, French Canada, and perhaps some sections in Southern Brazil where a German or Italian population prevails.

It is obvious that when we speak of inter-American relationships we must keep in mind this complex racial and cultural picture and not only the simple geographical scenery.

The several methods by which all these Americas were born must also be considered. These methods ran all the way from ruthless conquest to quiet immigration. In areas where the European invaders found only weak or sparsely settled Indian tribes, these original Americans were more or less rapidly exterminated or thrown out, and the remnants perhaps confined to reservations. This was the case in Canada, the Eastern United States, Cuba, Puerto Rico, Costa Rica, Uruguay, and partially so in Argentina. In other areas, the invaders ran up against strong and numerous Indian nations, and after a cruel conquest, a very large Indian population remained to be enslaved or pushed back into the jungle. This fact of the enslaved or wild Indian gave some of these newborn American nations special features and problems.

The need of laborers in those areas where the Indians were either extinct or not available, because they had either fled into the jungles or were still entrenched in their Western desert strongholds, resulted in the importation of African slaves by the millions. Here again, the fact of the enslaved Negro created special situations and difficulties for some of our countries.

Two different traditions entered into the making of the Americas. One was British and Protestant; the other, Portuguese or Spanish, and Roman Catholic. The Portuguese and Spanish adventure was in the strides of imperialism. Their kings wanted more lands under their feet and more riches for their coffers; their soldiers were thirsty for wealth and power; their colonists were in quest of easy and fabulous profit; their priests, with some noble and outstanding exceptions of real apostolic zeal, came primarily to claim new dominions for the power and glory of the church and to help consolidate the rule of its royal protectors. A despotic and fanatic rule was thus extended to the New World, giving its fatal taint to the culture evolved under its auspices, where so many fine elements were otherwise present.

On the other hand, the Pilgrim Fathers came to the northern shores of the New World seeking for freedom; not mere physical freedom, because they were not slaves, but freedom of worship, freedom of conscience, the most fundamental and precious of all freedoms. Although they thus escaped from British conformity, they were not at first desirous of detaching themselves from British rule, a rule that, in spite of all, had been influenced by a long-standing tradition of liberty and democracy. The "Mayflower's" voyage was not a venture of conquest and imperialism, although the Pilgrims had to fight the Indians in order to gain a foothold in the land. They were not interested in adding to the power and glory of the British Crown. And since they themselves had been the victims of intolerance and ecclesiastical monopoly, neither were they interested in bringing new territories under the thumb of the British church. It is true that they themselves were not always free from intolerance and fanaticism, but the general and inevitable trend in their colonies was that of freedom of conscience and democratic government. They became the classical lands of freedom and of a new start.

There was, therefore, an essential difference in the birth of the two main sections of the New World, a difference that accounts for most of the other differences and of the several problems involved in inter-American relationships today.

ELEMENTS IN MISUNDERSTANDING

It is no easy task to give a summary of the elements making for misunderstanding in inter-American relationships. They are deep, complex, and traditional. But at least we may mention those that seem to be more evident.

First of all, there is a traditional element inherited from the old struggles for power in Europe. The imperial Spain of Charles V and Philip II saw a dangerous rival in a growing imperial Great Britain. In the religious realm, Spain became the leader of the Counter Reformation, directing its might against the Reformation, whose forces had now become centered in England and Scotland. The idea of a manifest destiny to stop and overrule the Anglo-Saxons, considered as natural enemies, became embedded in the Spanish mind. The tendency to transplant the seeds of this conflict to the New World was irresistible, on both sides. Spain advanced its posts as far north as possible. The United States encouraged, along with Great Britain, the independence of the colonies from Spain, a process which culminated in the Spanish-American War and the loss by Spain of its last possessions in America and in the Far East.

The expanding power of the United States, west and south, during the first half of the last century, resulted in the loss, by Mexico, of more than half of its territory. This blow to a Spanish-American nation was deeply resented by all the countries to the south, not only in itself as an accomplished fact, but also as an indication of a certain menace hanging over all the rest of Spanish America. Although nearly a century has passed, that unfortunate happening is still alive as a source of resentment and distrust.

Selfish interests from the United States, allied with political corruption in Latin America, have at different times promoted a policy of economic domination and diplomatic or military intervention by the big Northern nation in the affairs of her sister republics. Racial prejudice on both sides has added fuel to aggressiveness, resentment, and distrust. The anxiety of the Roman Catholic church to maintain at all costs the monopoly of which it was legally deprived by the constitutions of most of the Latin-American coun-

139

tries, after they became independent from Spain and Portugal, has infused the situation with a dangerous element, that of religious fanaticism. Hostility toward the United States has thus been consistently encouraged in the name of religion.

The emigration of poor and uneducated Latin Americans seeking jobs and the stream southward of voracious prospectors and investors from the United States have given rise to the mind picture of the "typical" Latin American and the "typical" Anglo-American. For the Northern neighbors, the Latin American is either a "greaser" or a lazy daydreamer, the man of dirt and *manana* and ignorance; while, in retaliation, for the Southern neighbors, the Anglo-American is the arrogant "gringo," the business shark, scheming and planning all the time for economic exploitation of other countries, the man of money, amazing techniques, easy divorce, "wild oats," hypocrisy, and racial pride. The lack of true knowledge of each other and the tragic or funny mistakes in judgment that are thus made on both sides are now a commonplace and need not be stressed.

Differences in race, culture, tastes, character, and tradition have often been considered as in necessary opposition and conflict, as utterly incompatible, as divinely appointed to wage a relentless war between themselves until one succeeds in displacing the other. The idea of two worlds, two separate worlds, the Latin-American and the Anglo-American, impossible of any reconciliation, thus dominates the thinking and the attitudes of multitudes of people north and south

140

of the Rio Grande. The "they" and the "we" have achieved a fierce, aggressive meaning. Contempt and resentment have been too often left to rule our relationships.

THE TREND TOWARD INTER-AMERICAN UNION

It was a Latin American, the great Simon Bolivar, who first had a wide vision of a continental fellowship of nations. He is the real father of Pan-Americanism. He advocated a union of all the peoples of America, as the whole continent has been called always by Latin Americans. He had in mind a great confederation under a central government, "independent nations bound together by a common law," with a general and permanent congress "of all the American States." He planned the Congress of Panama, from which he expected "the largest, most extraordinary, and strongest League of Nations" to arise. He even outlined the fundamental principles of a real society of nations in his famous seven points: No war between the contracting parties; international law included in the legislation of each country; the abolition of slavery and other social reforms "under the holy auspices of liberty"; internal democratic organizations; sanctions against any member violating the fundamental principles of the confederation; the power of all states coming to the rescue of any victim of external aggression or internal disorders; a federal army and navy for the protection of all.

True it is that Bolivar was especially interested in the confederation of the republics just emancipated

141

from Spain. He frequently spoke of a Spanish-American league of nations. The United States were not included in his first proposals. But two considerations may help to understand him at this point. First, his Spanish-American confederation was not to be set as against the United States, on whose friendship he counted with particular stress, but against the imperialistic ambitions of Europe; second, his hesitation was due mainly to the desire not to offend Great Britain, whose friendship he also wished to retain, and of whose feelings toward the former British colonies of America he was not sure. He was afraid that the inclusion of the United States in this American confederation might arouse the suspicions and ill will of Great Britain. Therefore, he thought rather of a Spanish-American league of nations in the "most intimate and closest alliance with England and North America." But, as Mr. Luis Quintanilla has very forcefully proved, Bolivar seemed finally to have changed his mind in this regard, and he gave instructions to invite the United States to send delegates to the Panama Congress. "I am firmly persuaded," he wrote, "that none among the allies will fail to see with satisfaction those sincere and enlightened friends take part in our deliberations upon subjects referring to our common interests."[1]

Bolivar's plans failed. The Congress of Panama was poorly attended. Strong opposition was felt from all sides, including the United States and Great Brit-

[1] *A Latin American Speaks.* Copyright, 1943, by the Macmillan Co., publishers. Used by permission.

ain. Neither nation wanted, at that time, to indulge in any act which the European countries might interpret as a hostile policy toward them. Nevertheless, the dream of Bolivar disclosed the inner urge for inter-American union and laid down the broad fundamental principles for any such relationship in the future.

RISE AND DECLINE OF THE MONROE DOCTRINE

At the time when President Monroe made his famous declaration that the nations of the new continent were "not to be considered as subjects for future colonization by any European powers" and that "any attempt on their part to extend their system to any portion of this hemisphere" would be considered by the United States as "dangerous" to their "peace and security," it produced an excellent result. It was a warning to Europe that the independence of the weaker American nations was safeguarded by the strongest of them. Under the protection afforded by this doctrine, the Spanish-American and Portuguese-American republics had a respite from the menace of a reconquest and could therefore devote themselves to the consolidation and organization of their independent life.

But there is always danger in self-appointed guardianship, especially when, as was the case with Monroeism, the "peace and security" of the guardian rather than that of the guarded was made the first and determining consideration. Quite soon, the Mon-

143

roe Doctrine became, in practice, a claim to perennial supervision and a pretext for direct intervention on the part of the United States in the affairs of the other countries. An American of good faith always finds it difficult to understand why a doctrine affording protection to the Latin-American people has never been popular with them. But it is more difficult for Latin Americans to believe in the real protectiveness of a doctrine that has not interfered with such unfortunate happenings as the taking of Mexico's northern territories, of Puerto Rico, and the Panama Canal Zone, the forcing of the Platt Amendment upon Cuba, and the military interventions in Cuba, Haiti, Mexico, the Dominican Republic, and Nicaragua. The big question in Latin-American minds is always, "Protection, yes; but who is going to protect us against the protector?"

Gathering up the threads of the case against the Monroe Doctrine, as indicated not only by Latin-American but also by Anglo-American writers, Mr. Luis Quintanilla makes five charges: (1) It is *unilateral;* (2) it proved *inefficient;* (3) it was *perverted;* (4) it is *unpopular;* (5) it has become *outmoded.*[2] For the detailed arguments, readers are referred to his book.

One thing is clear. The Monroe Doctrine has long ago ceased to be, if it ever was (which is doubtful), an adequate code for inter-American relationships.

---

[2] *A Latin American Speaks,* p. 113. Used by permission of the Macmillan Co., publishers.

From "Big Stick" to "Good Neighbor" Policy

That the "big stick" could easily be hidden under the robes of the Monroe Doctrine may be considered as the last and decisive evidence against it. According to that classic policy, it was the "manifest destiny" of the United States to "introduce law and order" in the noisy, restless, backward nations to the south, by sheer force, swinging the "big stick" when necessary. No effort was made to understand the reasons for Latin-American troubles and to help solve them in a rational, constructive way. No recognition was given to the fact that often those troubles had been either created or used to their advantage by the same selfish interests, here in the United States, that requested the landing of the marines to "introduce law and order." Or still more than often, there seemed to be no awareness of the fact that the type of "law and order" these interests wanted was one which they would not have accepted for their own country, one which would allow to them alone the undisturbed exploitation of the other countries. "You must see to it that conditions are settled in those countries down there," these people said to the State Department, "so that we may be able to make safe and profitable investments in them."

"I took the Canal Zone," said Colonel Theodore Roosevelt in blunt honesty, when men in his administration were trying to prove to the world that a country recently become independent on its own accord, had freely and gladly presented the zone to the United States. The "big stick" people tried to develop a moral and international justification of armed intrusion. "We need it; we just take it, be the justice of it as it may." This is the same doctrine that the totalitarian powers hold today.

But if a policy that left so deep perturbations in inter-American relationships was associated with one Roosevelt, it is another Roosevelt who is associated with the great shift of policy, a shift that seems to be, and we Latin Americans hope it actually is, a real conversion. It was President Wilson who started the shift. But he was still a man of transition, caught to a certain extent in the wheels of a policy of outright and undiscriminating protection of vested interests, and so, in spite of his idealism, he was pushed to order the military intervention in Mexico. For a different action, more in accordance with his personal desires, he lacked, as in several other matters, enough support from his people. President Roosevelt has been more able and also has found himself placed in a better situation to carry a new policy into practical application. The people of the United States are now better prepared to understand it; Latin America is also better disposed to accept and trust the friendship of the "Colossus of the North." The tragic experiences of the last and the present war have helped both sides to see what a fatal mistake it is to quarrel or stay away from each other. Thus, in several ways, we are now witnessing how Wilsonian idealism becomes Rooseveltian realism, to the advantage of both parties.

146

But even this Good Neighbor policy, in its present stage, is still tainted by the evils of financial and political stress. It has to be expanded and deepened. It must be infused with profound moral and spiritual motivations. Also, it must not remain unilateral. More and more, it must become a continental policy heartily accepted and practiced by all and as purified as it may be of selfish convenience and hypocrisy, evils to which both sides are liable. Finally, it must have a wide meaning and application. The problem is not only that of Latin America as over against Anglo-Saxon America. If we ourselves, in the preceding paragraphs, have dwelt on this dual statement of the issue, it is merely because it constitutes its main aspect. But it is not the only one. We must keep in mind that there are several Americas, as we said in the beginning, and that conflicts and frictions exist between all of them. There is a problem of good relationships between the Latin-American nations among themselves. There is also a problem of Indian America and of Negro America in their relationships to the rest.

Therefore, the Good Neighbor policy, as stated and carried out at present, is splendid, but not enough. Here is the point where a Christian view of inter-American relationships becomes not only useful but imperative and indispensable.

A CHRISTIAN VIEW OF NATIONS

We find in the Old Testament, especially in the Prophets, some basic elements of the Christian view

147

of the nation. The fact that different nations exist
is not only given recognition, but generally conceived
as a divine order. God is the supreme ruler of nations. He establishes them according to his design
and sets their limits and, as Paul said to the Athe-
nians, their "appointed seasons," the time of their
rise and of their decline. The view that the boundary
lines between nations are always divinely drawn is,
of course, a concept that cannot strictly be carried
into the Christian view. We know that often boundaries are established by the designs of men, by wanton
attack on other nations, by deceit and cunningness
and by arbitrary decisions based on mere power and
national ambitions. And yet the truth that the old
seers of Israel and Paul wanted to stress in a language that need not be applied too literally is that
nations are in the hands of the Lord, that they are
subject to a divine law, that nations are not absolute,
determining their destiny for themselves purely according to their own wit and whim. *There is a moral
law, God's law, to which nations, the same as individual men, must submit*—a law of justice which is
above the sovereignty of the individual states and
their rulers. "First the Kingdom of God and its
justice," is the Christ-given criterion of values and
priorities. International law must find its source,
therefore, not in any balance of power or any purely
human contract, but in this divine law of justice.
This was the solid ground on which prophets and
apostles stood when they uttered their ringing and

fearless denunciations of kings and rulers, nations and peoples, who ran against that divine law.

This Christian concept of a divine moral law above the nation involves the complete repudiation of Machiavellianism, the theory that each nation is its own law and that this law should be imposed upon other nations by the use of power and political wit, a moral anarchy that results in international chaos or ruthless imperialism.

The Christian view also involves the recognition of divine vocations for all nations. He has bestowed gifts upon every nation, but they carry an inherent responsibility. They are not intended merely as special favors, but are the token of and the equipment for the fulfillment of a divine commission. Power, wealth, influence, cultural richness, as we know only too well, are not ends in themselves. "Chosen peoples" are not pet children, but rather peoples selected by God, like men at the front chosen for special duty by their commander, to sally forth and undertake an important and often dangerous and sacrificial task. But the fact that some are especially chosen for definite duties does not exclude the others from God's plans and assignments. Israel was the Lord's "chosen people," and yet the prophets could have the Lord speak of Cyrus and Nebuchadnezzar as His "servants." This means that no nation is ever deprived of a divine vocation, and that therefore no nation is void of gifts and possibilities.

This consideration leads us to our third point with regard to a Christian view of nations. *The worth of a nation depends, essentially, upon its divine vocation and, practically, upon the extent to which it is willing and able to fulfill that vocation.* And since the Lord has a vocation for all and each of the nations, our conclusion is that there is no nation, be it large or small, rich or poor, strong or weak, culturally advanced or backward, that is worthless or of very little worth. The dignity of nations, as the dignity of individual human personalities, becomes thus one of the great assertions of the Christian faith. The Lord who extends his concern to the least of a tree's leaves, should he not be tenderly concerned over the least of the nations? The worth of a nation is rooted in this divine concern and in the vocation it involves; it is up to the nation only to bring its vocation to full accomplishment or to frustrate it by evil-doing. Only in this truly Christian sense of the supremacy of obedience to God's will and of service are we allowed to speak of superior and inferior nations. Otherwise, there are no inferior nations. And indeed there are no *permanently* or *naturally* inferior nations. Race, wealth, military might, political power, territorial extension, size of population, do not, in themselves, make a nation superior. Jesus' judgment is final: "And whichever of you wishes to become first in rank shall be bound to serve you all."

The fourth great assertion in a Christian view of nations is that differences do not necessarily involve a hierarchy of value or opposition and conflict. God created all men and nations equal in their essential nature and worth, but widely different in other respects. His design of the universe, "the mystery of His will," as Paul puts it, seems not to be that of a gray uniformity but that of a great variety in individual differences, all being caught up into a perfect unity, "that in the dispensation of the fulness of times he might gather together in one all things in Christ, both which are in heaven, and which are on earth." Natural differences in themselves do not make some nations superior and others inferior. They are simply different. A difference may be an advantage when the conditions are also different. A dark skin, for instance, is a distinct protection in latitudes under a tropical sun. It may have even a beauty of its own. And, incidentally, this may explain the white people's present fashion of getting their skin tanned on the beach or under expensive quartz sun lamps. The same may be true of intellectual or temperamental inclinations and peculiarities. It is very naïve to interpret every difference we find in other people as an infallible sign of their inferiority or superiority.

Differences, again, do not necessarily involve antagonism. Differences may become, in the last analysis, supplementary. God distributed his gifts among all peoples and nations. It may have been his purpose that, in the finding by each of a sense of incompleteness, all might get closer together and try to share what they have in order to supplement each other. Latin Americans are poets, and Anglo-Americans engineers, as Dr. Samuel Guy Inman has put it; Latin Americans are Don Quixotes, and Anglo-

Americans Robinson Crusoes, as Dr. John A. Mackay expresses the difference. Well, let them not quarrel over the superior value of their gifts. Let them get together and put themselves to a common task. After all, poets must work hard, and engineers must dream; Don Quixote must become resourceful and practical, and Robinson Crusoe must abandon his isolation and take time from his business and try to help right the wrongs, free the captives, and straighten the world up. But not all are differences either. Besides differences, there are close affinities. After all, we were all made from the same clay. There is a common human heritage, simply human. By merging our affinities and harmonizing our differences, instead of ignoring the former and unwisely stressing the latter, thus heading for trouble, we of the Americas and of all nations may work together toward the realization of God's purpose, finding in this common purpose and this common goal the strongest tie of brotherhood, justice, and peace.

Several important corollaries for inter-American relationships follow when this fourfold Christian view of nations is applied.

The Right of Self-Determination

Man is spirit. And one of the essential qualities of a spirit is freedom. The right of self-determination for groups of men thus becomes a birthright, a natural and spiritual gift from God. Nothing can be more contrary to the Christian gospel than oppression and bondage. The liberation of Israel in the

Old Testament, the passionate longings of the Exile prophets for liberty, are not only historical facts but are also true parables of the divine will. Jesus begins his ministry with a clarion call to freedom, in the words of the old seer of his people: "The Spirit of the Lord is upon me, because he hath anointed me to preach the gospel to the poor; . . . to preach deliverance to the captives, . . . to set at liberty them that are bruised." The gospel is here identified with the freedom of captives and the liberty of them that are bruised and downtrodden. And it is no less than the Spirit of the Lord that compels men to preach and to seek liberty.

This proclamation by Jesus is the basic Christian Magna Charta of all liberties. Our sad tendency to water down the revolutionary force of the gospel is reflected in our having given this Scripture an exclusively spiritual interpretation. But, as Dr. E. Stanley Jones has so ably shown, not only spiritual liberty—freedom from the bondage of sin—is here involved; but also economic liberty, freedom from want; social and political liberty, the right of self-determination, true democracy; physical liberty, freedom from disease, the right to healthy living. The Four Freedoms, so forcefully and distinctly placed by President Roosevelt as the United Nations' goal today, have not gone beyond the scope of that splendid comprehensive Christian program.

Not all the American nations are free. Some are still under political bondage. Most of them are under economic servitude. In a few of them, freedom of conscience, freedom of worship, is having a hard time to subsist. In all of them, racial and social prejudice is in one way or another closing the doors of opportunity for millions of people. Inter-American relationships must be definitely based, not only on the recognition by all of the right to freedom by all, but more than that—if the Christian view is to be applied —on the principle of special help to those nations and communities that they may achieve a fuller freedom. The American family of peoples must see to it that all and every one of its members shall develop into a full-grown, self-governing, free, and progressive nation. In order to be permanent and fruitful, inter-American relationships must be freely undertaken. True and sound relationships can be established only among free nations.

EQUAL RIGHTS AND OBLIGATIONS

Every time a Pan-American conference meets, it is only natural that the question of rights and obligations should become foremost in the discussions. The Latin-American countries are still suspicious that some of their essential rights might become cramped if they tie themselves up in international obligations. Unfortunately, stronger nations have always shown a tendency to get the lion's share in all international agreements. Naturally, the weaker nations shrink from real cooperation lest their condition be that of mere tools in the hands of the powerful.

The recognition of equal rights and obligations is basic in sound relationships. And we may congratulate ourselves that the Americas are making progress in that direction. But more than a mere recognition is necessary. The shadows of the past are still thick and wide. Guarantees must be given that this recognition shall be actually carried over into practice. There are many instances where a verbal recognition serves only to camouflage a practical denial.

So far, such a recognition is a matter of pure common sense and natural law. The Christian view goes still further. It stresses the fact that all exercise of rights involves an acceptance of obligations. No right without obligations. No obligation without rights. Considering themselves menaced by the stronger nations, it is only natural that the weaker nations should stress their rights. They must be helped to see that once their rights are safeguarded, they must be ready to assume their obligations in exchange. On the other hand, the Christian view insists that greatness, power, and wealth involve larger and special obligations. A stronger nation must be ready to accept a larger responsibility. The more one has, the more one is bound to give. In the third place, the Christian view involves the principle that sometimes it is necessary, for the sake of others, to limit one's own exercise of rights. It is not a question of *being deprived* of a right; it is a question of *voluntarily giving up* the full exercise of certain rights for the sake of good relationships. It is the sacrificial principle at work.

No other policy than that of good will carried to the sacrificial point, the policy of the second mile, will ever enable the stronger nations to win back the trust and confidence of the weaker nations. Is this a hard word for the stronger nations to hear? Yes, some words in the Christian gospel are very hard to hear. As many of the disciples once said, "This is a hard saying; who can hear it?" But it is the only word that can succeed in wiping away resentment and in straightening up inter-American relationships. A cold stop at the strict limit of an obligation will never achieve that.

OPPORTUNITY FOR SELF-DEVELOPMENT

Over a year ago, I stood in the office of one of the largest shipbuilding companies in this country. Another "liberty ship" had just been launched. I was in conversation with the president of the company. We talked about war production and of the possible cooperation of Mexico and the other Latin-American allies. "In your opinion," I asked, "what is the role of Latin America in the defense of our continent?" The answer came straight back, "To produce raw materials, plenty of raw materials, for us." "Yes," I said, "I guess that is one of the things we should do." "That is the one important thing you should do," he insisted. Then I tried to express our feeling that the situation of a country limited to the production of raw materials is always an inferior one, that it becomes practically an economic colony of the highly industrialized countries, because it sees itself forced, first, to sell its raw materials at any price and then to buy them back, along with other

156

materials, in their manufactured form, also at any price. "You must help us," I said, "to improve our production of raw materials, but also to become industrial countries ourselves. Economic freedom is possible for a country only when it becomes capable of industrializing its own resources and does not have to beg by the roadside for somebody to buy them." But the gentleman did not agree. "Look at the Dutch Indies," he said. "How prosperous they have been, and they were producers only of raw materials!" The picture came to my mind of the prosperous Dutch colonists and the thousands of miserable coolies roasting their bare backs, bent under the tropical sun. The president of the company had given away his case by citing a precise example of a colony, not of a free land.

This incident illustrates the kind of economic relationships that many people still consider consistent with good will and true cooperation. The United States, I am sure, would never have accepted the position of a mere producer of raw materials for the English factories and a mere market for English goods. That they did not do so accounts not only for the fact that this country has so marvelously developed, but also for the fact that it has thus been able to come to the rescue of Great Britain, in this hour of peril, with all the strength of its huge industrial plants.

In its economic aspect, inter-American relationships must give all the Americas a real opportunity for full development. Only when all the Americas become economically strong, and therefore capable of mutual assistance, will relationships be satisfactory. A weak Latin America used to be the ideal of enterprising Anglo-Americans, because it was easier to exploit and dominate. A situation of permanent inferiority for the Indians and the Negroes has also been considered as essential to avoid their giving *us* trouble. We are now discovering the big blunder of that policy. Large masses of population, held in an inferior condition, hamper the progress of the whole nation. In the hour of crisis, a weak Latin America becomes either a cracking wall for the assault of the enemy or an expensive charge. In both cases, interracially and internationally, that policy has become a fearful boomerang.

The extending of all possible help to the weaker nations in order to assist them to stand on their own feet and become economically strong and fully developed is sheer sound economic policy. From a Christian viewpoint it is simply the courageous application of the Golden Rule. We have mentioned here the economic side only, because it is the most apparent at the present time. But of course, self-development includes much more than that. Social, intellectual, and spiritual development is basic. In all these matters the concern of all should be that no one among them shall forever remain in an undeveloped condition. It is for the good of all that all shall become as fully developed as possible. Inter-American relationships, under a Christian view, must not be a paternalistic or oppressive rule of the stronger, but a cooperation in brotherhood, where everyone is pledged to assist all the rest to achieve the fullest possible development.

But it is essential that this development be interpreted finally in terms of moral and spiritual character. Mere economic development will bring the American nations to a clash, unless it is subordinated to moral and spiritual principle. Although it is possible, out of bare convenience, to bring economic interests to a certain degree of adjustment and cooperation, they always carry in themselves the seeds of competition and strife. True cooperation is always the offspring of high moral and spiritual character.

GREATNESS IS A MORAL AND SPIRITUAL VALUE

We come thus to another point in our Christian program. The true greatness of a country lies in its moral and spiritual resources. Once and again we have seen a nation almost deprived of its wealth rise up against all odds and come to its feet again. This is the miracle of character. But sometimes this miracle is faked by pride, hate, and resentment. But these elements, although able to perform the feat— as in the case of Germany—always blow it to its own destruction. It is for nations, wishing to apply the Christian principles to their life, to demonstrate that kindness, love, forgiveness, plus intelligence and hard work, can perform a more permanent and real miracle. In seeking that greatness of character, not only for oneself but also for the others, the Americas shall be able to build a great continental family of nations.

It therefore becomes imperative to exterminate national pride and national resentment. The Anglo-American nations, so powerful and progressive, may yield to the temptation of exclusiveness, pride, and the superiority complex, while the rest may indulge in the sordid comfort of an eternal hatred of them. We must confess that these elements have been very active until now. They have to a very large extent determined inter-American relationships and shaped the history of our continent. A Christian view urges the immediate turning away from this and summons the Christians in all the Americas to the sacrificial task of doing away with it completely.

The Foundation of Interdependence

When Paul said, referring to the Christian converts, that "we are members one of another," he was not only expressing a law in the mystic realm of the church, but also a fact in the natural realm of nations and of their relationships with one another. This is the fact of interdependence. That we live in a shrinking world is now a commonplace. The Americas are still more closely bound together by their common dwelling on this continent. Not only are modern communications bringing them closer and closer, but the very nature of modern life is making one people depend increasingly on the others for the enjoyment of its commodities. Our food, our clothing, many of the various things we cannot dispense with in our daily round, travel a long way to come to us and represent the intelligence and labor of people of many nations whom we may never see or know about. This is more particularly true of the nations of our continent, as at present illustrated with great force, when supplies from other continents are practically cut off.

Peace, justice, and welfare are indivisible. No nation can possibly enjoy them in full when far or near there are other nations deprived of them. Injustice, unrest, suffering, want, all the evils of social and national disease, cannot be kept strictly within the limits of any one country or community. They have a tendency to spread like physical disease. They poison the air for all. Their subtle, mortiferous germs travel wide and fast and reach even those who, in luxurious isolation, feel themselves secure and immune. Unrest, poverty, oppression, ignorance, in the neighbor nations: none of my business? Let them see to it by themselves? Such an attitude is not only morally unsound but practically impossible to hold to. Sooner or later the misery and suffering of my neighbor creeps under my own gate, filters through the very troubleproof screen of my front door, or jumps over the fence into my back yard, sneaks into my cellar, and finally pervades my whole house. The world has been learning a very hard lesson, a double lesson. First, that the idea that I can be spared when my neighbor is being abused, simply because I shrug my shoulders and put up above my roof the banner of neutrality, is a stupid and fatal delusion. Second, that a nation cannot enjoy peace when it is based on a policy of keeping

the rest at each other's throat, on the theory that
they will be too busy to prevent their pockets being
picked or to disturb our own peace. It is particularly
the second lesson that many in the Americas still
have to learn. The traditional policy of vested interests in the stronger nations has been to keep the
weaker nations, often even by the employment of
provoking agents, in a state of internal strife or of
conflict with the others. The case of the oil interests
that were paying a rebel army against the Mexican
Government in 1919, as fearlessly denounced by an
American newspaperman, Mr. L. J. de Bekker, is
only one instance of this policy. We have never
become convinced in Latin America that similar interests did not foment the Chaco war between Bolivia
and Paraguay or have had nothing to do with the
perennial conflict between Peru and Ecuador.

Inter-American relationships, if they are to be
genuine and permanent, must be generously built
upon the foundation of interdependence. Self-sufficient nationalism must be relentlessly denounced as
a suicidal policy. "We are members one of another."
The peace, justice, security, and welfare of everyone
must become the sacrificial concern of all. The pattern for relationships in this regard may be given
in the words of Paul: "But now are they many members, yet but one body. And the eye cannot say unto
the hand, I have no need of thee: nor again the head
to the feet, I have no need of you. Nay, much more
those members of the body, which seem to be more
feeble, are necessary. . . . That there should be no

schism in the body; but that the members should have the same care one for another.''

The Policy of Mutual Assistance

The fact of interdependence calls for the policy of mutual assistance. It is very easy for a strong nation to conceive, by the very abundance of its resources, of many ways in which it can bestow them on the less privileged ones. It is more difficult for that same nation to conceive of some ways in which the weaker nations may assist in their turn, or to admit that it needs their assistance. On the other hand, it is very easy for a weak nation to adopt the attitude of the ''respectable pauper,'' to consider it the duty of only the stronger nations to render their talents and to retreat into a condition of passivism, of pessimism regarding its own possibilities, and of despondency. It is more difficult for that same nation to find that it may also contribute something to the welfare of all, that it can give help to those who are still in a lower situation, and that it can, in a sense, pay for the assistance it is receiving by what it does for those less fortunate than itself.

The principle of mutual assistance must be accepted by both sides. No nation is ever so utterly deprived of gifts that there is really nothing that it can share with the others. Mutual assistance means sharing the best each has, the protection of everyone by all, and the support of all by everyone, special help to the weakest, continuous service like a golden stream flowing to and fro.

There is a good deal of inter-American assistance today, on account of the war. In this time of crisis, practically no one would dare to run against the evidence that we need each other. Hard-boiled isolationists all along the continent are beginning to see that the ties between the American nations work both ways. There remains, however (and I have heard it voiced in my own and in this country often), a certain idea that all this fine cooperation may be a mere emergency measure, another expedient made necessary by the war, something, in brief, that will disappear once the war is over and the urge of sheer necessity stops or political administrations shift.

It is for us Christians to help this principle to take deeper roots in our peoples, so that besides being a policy of our administrations, it may become ingrained in the very soul of the masses and a permanent policy in our relationships. It is for us Christians also to help to discover new and more extensive ways of making this assistance effective. Finally, it is for us to inspire it with the true spirit of friendship, so that whatever political shifts may come, it shall remain strong and always above the level of selfish interest.

The Realism of the Golden Rule

There has been always a tendency to place international relationships outside the sphere where the Christian principles hold good. It is often claimed that moral laws have to do only with the individual man, and that it is impossible to apply them to the behavior of nations and states. But this claim is especially emphatic with regard to Christian ethics. Even many Christians are pessimistic on this matter and join forces with those who profess the impossibility of accepting a Christian international law. Without entering fully into this discussion, we may say that if the principles of Christian ethics are summarized, for practical purposes, in the Golden Rule, there has been no time in history when the realism of that principle, as applied to international relationships, has been more evident.

A nation has been mistreated. Entire populations in a subject country have been held in submission. Racial minorities have been oppressed. Opportunity for full development has been denied to those areas assigned by economic imperialism as permanent producers of raw materials and consumers of manufactured goods. Threats and aggression have been the favorite methods of intimidating the weak into agreements and combinations to their detriment. Then, war breaks out. These populations, minorities, and areas make the desperate decision to throw themselves into the arms of the common enemy, just because their only hope seems to be in a change of masters. They resort either to quiet noncooperation or to active sabotage. Their former lords get a stab in their backs. Other populations have been, on the contrary, treated with relative kindness and assisted to develop into self-government. When war comes, these people stand bravely by their friends and protectors. They may not be completely satisfied with them, but they at least realize on which side are their best hope and chance. This is hardheaded realism, is it not? Well, this is exactly what the Golden Rule means. "And as ye would that men should do to you, do ye also to them likewise." This is a policy that carries in itself its own reward. It is not wishful thinking. It is sound political realism.

It is for us Christians of the Americas to help lift up the Golden Rule from the purely individual level to the realm of international relationships.

NEW MEN FOR THE NEW DAY

When the Christian view is applied, when as a result the family pattern of international relationships becomes our guide and goal, then a new day looms on the horizon. And the stars of the morning raise their song of joy. You can build a new machine with scrap iron, but you can never build a new world with scraps of the "old man," of the men who are not capable of becoming kindled with the fire of a new spirit. You need new men for a new day. And by new men, we mean not only another generation but also a generation with a changed heart. The stress of the Christian gospel, when dealing with programs to rebuild the world, is that the essential change must take place in the inner self, in men's hearts, and not merely in outward conditions.

We not only need, then, to set the Christian view of international relationships as an ideal before our politicians and statesmen, our leaders and peoples; we need, above all, Christian action. The main task of the Christian churches today becomes again the production of men with a changed heart. If production has become the key word for victory and post-war reconstruction, then we Christians must enter the race for production too: the production of Christian men and women, the best materials for the building of a new international structure.

This means that for us Christians, Pan-Americanism or inter-Americanism is not enough. At no point is a real conversion of heart more needed, because there are still many "converted" Christians who, in their international thinking, are nothing less than petrified heathens. It is here that our evangelistic work assumes an international importance. Because it is only the power of the liberating Christ in the heart that can wipe out pride, resentment, and selfishness. Then these *truly converted* Christians, by organizing themselves for public action through education, literature, and honest politics, may come to be a decisive influence in guiding our international relationships into a Christian channel, not for the glory, power, or worldly influence of any church, but for the welfare and happiness of the Americas and of the *world*—of the world, because after all, to transcend national isolationism merely to fall into the pit of a meager Pan-American isolationism would again be a terrible mistake.

We in the Americas are not set up against the rest of the world. The great Simon Bolivar, who once dreamed of a strong and united continent, was, in spite of his anti-European bias, great enough to see a larger, higher vision. He had, as one of his biographers has said, "a cosmic conscience." "Perhaps," Bolivar said, caught up in the fires of prophecy, "in the march of centuries, one Nation alone—the Federal Nation—will embrace the universe."

Our idea, therefore, in settling our inter-American relationships in such a way—the Christian way—and in such a spirit—the spirit of Christ—in order to build the Americas into a greater, happier, stronger family of nations, must be thus to become more able to render a larger service to the world, to the universal family of nations. In achieving this purpose, we find in the Christian view, although not a fixed pattern or blueprint, the highest inspiration and ideal; and in Christian action, although not infallible nor perfect nor omnipotent, the most effective and precious tool.

PEACE BEGINS AT HOME

Cleo W. Blackburn

PEACE begins at home; in your town and my town, in your church and my church, in your heart and my heart. Perhaps this seems to you an oversimplification, engaged as we are in the most terrifying war of all history, a war in which millions of men and billions of dollars and all the untold resources of the earth are being thrown together for the purpose of victory—a military victory designed to bring peace to the world. Yet this war, like all other wars, cannot bring peace. For peace is not born of war.

If a peaceful world is to be built after this war, it must be built within *us*. We ourselves must want peace. And more than that, we must be willing to pay the price of peace.

The great technical mobilization for total world war on the part of America has demonstrated one of the greatest miracles in the whole history of modern civilization. Never before has a great nation totally unprepared for war mobilized its energy and its resources to the point of peak production in such a short time. The other nations of the world have been dazzled by our great technical skills and the great genius of our industrial enterprise. Yes, we have paid the price for military victory: tanks, planes, guns, young men, blood plasma, supplies, communication, and transportation. Victory on the battlefield is ours. Of course, there is much fighting ahead—bloody fighting, the worst the world has ever seen. Yet we are now fully confident that success is within our grasp.

After this war the United States of America will emerge the strongest military power the world has ever seen—a fleet estimated at some thirty-five to forty thousand ships, a half million to a million airplanes, and industrial plants the like of which the world has never seen. Because of this, America stands the chance of becoming the most feared nation in the world, the nation to make alliances against, the nation which perhaps will play the same role in the world family of nations that Germany has played in the last seventy-five or one hundred years, a great power which threatens the security of the other great powers of the world, a power which perhaps will become suspected and mistrusted by many of the lesser powers. Yes, we have paid the price of military victory, but the price of victory is not the price of peace.

The price of peace includes justice, good will, fair play, security for ourselves and for others. Two years ago America was caught wholly unprepared for total war. Today the American people are equally unprepared for peace. Our recent experiences in Spain, in North Africa, and in Italy indicated the extent of our unpreparedness.

The question arises, Do we really want peace and are we willing to pay the price for peace? Dr. Arthur E. Morgan has stated an answer in these words:

> If the conditions necessary to enduring peace should be clearly presented and clearly understood in America, I believe that a very consider-

able part of our population would feel that, convenient and pleasant as peace would be, occasional war would be preferable. If on the one hand our country could be thoroughly convinced that the present war would probably last ten years, that it would cost the lives of five millions of our sons and brothers, and the lives of five to ten times as many citizens of other nations and that the tax on our own and world resources would be correspondingly heavy; and if on the other hand we were convinced that we could now have enduring peace by paying the necessary price for it, I believe that many Americans of all classes would reject the conditions of peace and would choose war as the lesser evil.

This is actually the condition and position of many in America and England today. We want the comfortable, emotional feeling that enduring peace will follow this war. To feel that we had refused the condition of peace and so had made other wars certain would shock our self-respect.

If we should face realistically the actual price of lasting peace, the conditions would seem so undesirable to us that we could not bring ourselves to accept them. So we are shocked at the question and perhaps feel outraged when anyone forces it upon our attention. We lose our temper and our poise and immediately attempt to discredit the person who has sufficient courage to face the facts.

The fact is that the price of enduring peace is very high. No great nation, neither ours nor any other, is ready today to pay that price. That price is the guarantee of a chance at life for every man or association

of men and of every race of people, and that their
standing among men shall not depend on any entrenched position, prestige, power, race, color, property, or possession, but shall depend only on their willingness and their ability under fair and impartial opportunity to contribute to the progress and welfare
of mankind.

I fear that too many people do not understand the
basic causes of this war. This is no politician's war,
it is no banker's war, but it is a people's war and must
be seen in the light of its larger implications which go
much deeper than the apparent issues about which
battles are waged. This war reflects a breakdown in
the basic culture of our time. Our very way of life,
our whole sense of values, morals, our philosophy, our
religion, are all tied up in this war. This is revolution
—revolution and war at the same time. Not only is
our military might being tested, but also our moral
right to leadership in the world is being challenged.

America and her allies are being seen in bold relief
against a backdrop which is the world. Not only are
the great struggles being seen in terms of a wealth of
mechanical and technical skills and all the strength
which they represent, but also here the great weaknesses are being seen—the great lack of moral courage
and spiritual strength. Nobody doubts the power of
our young men and our military equipment to win this
war. Whether or not our leaders, our old men of fifty
or sixty, will have the moral courage to build a peace
is open to serious question. Do we even dare to speak
of a proper peace, we who send our men to battle on

the chief psychological and spiritual diet of glamour girls and smutty humor?

The so-called Four Freedoms are even plaguing us at home, their fallacies becoming increasingly obvious in New York, Boston, Detroit, and Beaumont. They will also become increasingly obvious in your town and in my town as the months go by.

One had only to listen to that remarkable keynote speech of the Republican National Committee meeting in Chicago a few weeks ago to realize that the politicians have not yet properly discerned what this war is about. Either that, or they are refusing to let themselves think about the elements and forces which must go into the making of the peace. But need I mention that meeting? Let us look toward Washington. Is the necessity to win a political campaign, either by Democrats or Republicans, so much more important that winning a lasting peace for the world?

Some of us have been shocked so many times these last two years that we are almost beyond shocking. We have seen political consideration time and time again take precedence of the best interests of the nation. We have seen our Congress lose countless hours bickering among themselves and struggling with the administration over petty, partisan matters. It may truly be said that one of the characteristics of our government during this period is government by confusion. The present war has not united us as a nation. If industry, as represented by labor and management, or any branch of our armed forces, had per-

173

formed in a similar manner we should be facing military disaster today.

The behavior of our political leaders, however, would not seem nearly so tragic if it were not so typically American. Their votes have been recorded and are reported both in the press and on the radio and still there has not been any spontaneous uprising of American citizens to protest. The most articulate cries have been those from special interest groups whose immediate or long-range selfish interest has been challenged or affected. Be it the National Association of Manufacturers, labor, the farmers, racial, civic, or religious minorities, each has cried out in its own selfish interest. There has yet to appear a great unified cry representing all groups championing the cause of decency and justice in America and in the world.

Our political leaders are simply reflecting the basic desires of the American people. They are reflecting the general hate neurosis which is plaguing all America. The salvation of the world does not rest in the hands of Franklin Roosevelt, or Winston Churchill, or Joseph Stalin, or Chiang Kai-shek. And hate will not disappear with Hitler, or Tojo, or Mussolini.

It is so easy to look to the top for help, or to personify our hate. Our crisis is reflected in our own way of life—in our own politics, our own economy, our own philosophy, our own art, our own religion, and our own morals. The Christian or the Jew has no pharisaic escape in the church or the synagogue. The church and the synagogue must bear their full responsibility. So many who call themselves Christians are

174

suffering from the same hate neurosis and participate actively, or even by their silence, in the hate pattern.

Of course, there are individuals, individual Christians and individual Jews, and small groups here and there who are giving themselves with all the strength and vigor they have that men may be free, that justice may prevail, and that the Kingdom of God may come.

Christianity has not failed, it has merely been found too difficult. It has not been tried. It has been compromised and rationalized to meet the so-called needs and to preserve the so-called values of society, needs and values which are not Christian, but largely imperialistic and nationalistic. If Christianity is lost to this generation, it will not be lost because of any outward evil influence, but it will be lost by default—lost in your town and in my town, in your church and my church, in your heart and my heart—all because we lack the simple, moral courage to make it work.

We have had entirely too much talk of justice, too many words about democracy, too much praying for peace, and we have provided none of the works which make peace possible.

Is it not obvious that we are no longer looking for a real peace? Is it not true that every national or special interest group is interested in winning the war to preserve the same kind of society we have always had, the kind of society which breeds war and hate, which talks Christianity, but does not practice it? The majority of us want to approach this situation with our same old forms of accounting, our same old methods of bookkeeping, our same old ideas and ideologies. We are still seeing the world through our own complexes. We have little conception of a peace involving all the peoples of the world. We are concerned about our own freedom, our own way of life, but too few of us are willing to give ourselves for the liberation and freedom of all oppressed peoples. This is not only true of the oppressor, it is also true of the oppressed.

As a member of a minority group, I am convinced that American Negroes must concern themselves not only with their own liberty and their own freedom, but that they must work for freedom as the lot of every human being. Our fight for freedom must go beyond our own suffering, for then and then only will it become a part of the great spiritual struggle for freedom in the world. If ours is to be a cheap fight just to save our own skins, only to free ourselves from discrimination and injustice, if our freedom is to be won at the expense of anyone else's freedom, it will not be a freedom which can last and bring security. But if ours is to be a struggle for freedom for all mankind, then freedom and justice will be ours!

But we may as well face the facts. Utopia will not follow this war. We may get a world army to prevent aggression for a few years, but you cannot make peace with armies. Peace is made in the hearts and lives of people—people in your town and in my town, people like you and like me.

The sad truth is that the issues of the third world war are being decided this very minute in our own home towns. For what can the national pattern be but the fusing of our own local community folkways?

Before America can point out to the world the way of good will, mutual regard, and mutual respect between white and colored people, we must have found such a way in the day-by-day life of our own home community. Unless Negro and white neighbors can learn to share opportunity and life with equality and without discrimination because of color, unless they can learn to worship God together in the same church, how can we say to the peoples of the world that we believe in democracy?

We in America have had the opportunity to demonstrate to the world that people of different races and different cultures and different religions and different economic levels can solve the problem of living together as equals in mutual respect for each other's differences. When we fail, then, in our local communities, what hope is there for peace among nations where these same differences exist?

Peace begins at home. And where is the beginning? It must begin by changing our basic attitude, our basic conception of ourselves, and our role in the world. The myths must go; the "black herring," poverty, isolationism and nationalism, the economy of scarcity. We must build a new ideology and a new frame of reference around which to organize our lives. We must end the old, old story of exploitation and arbitrary superiority.

Let us stop deluding ourselves. We are not deceiving anyone with our hypocrisy, with our words of

177

peace and brotherly love, by our vocal devotion to
democracy. Our works are too plainly seen.

When will we learn that our people must be given
a new perspective? That they must learn about other
people and other people's interests and cultures; no,
not to adopt them, but to understand them and appreciate them. With the destruction of the sense of
separateness and difference and with a growing community and oneness which is the world, a larger perspective for men in their separate communities becomes possible.

But you are interested in a real peace, you say.
What, then, are the mechanisms and the requirements? Dr. Eduard C. Lindeman, the great social
philosopher, has suggested three areas which should
be brought to the attention of the American people.
He said that, in the first place, the American ought to
be faced with the facts and asked point-blank questions. I shall repeat his direct questions.

> One: Are you ready to stand by this govern-
> ment's commitments in the postwar world? Such
> commitments as the Atlantic Charter? the United
> Nations agreement? the Moscow agreement?
> Cairo? Teheran?
> Two: Are you ready to face the postwar need
> for the four-power alliance of the United States,
> Great Britain, Russia, and China as the govern-
> ing board in the interim period?
> Three: Are you ready to extend the instru-
> ments of the present war into the peace? The
> lend-lease arrangement? The United Nations Re-

lief organization? The Board of Economic Warfare, changed to perhaps the Board of Economic
Peace? And all the other vital agencies?

Some further questions might be added: Are we
ready to put an end to tariff barriers—at least on
such things as drugs and medical supplies? Are we
ready to go on record that we shall require no special
privileges for ourselves that we are not willing to
grant to other people? That, indeed, the nonrestric-
tion on raw materials suggested in the Atlantic Charter shall be one of the primary requisites for peace?
That racial equality shall be one of the primary requisites?

How many of these requisites are the people of
your community ready to face? How many are they
willing to accept? How much effort are they willing
to put into educational programs to see that America
does fulfill her obligation to the building of a just
peace?

The people are ready to talk about these things.
Our great problem is not the people, but the leaders.
For the leaders of the people, including their religious
leaders, are afraid to face the truth.

The problem is whether we can inspire our present
leadership to meet the challenge. Can we look to the
present leadership of the church to stimulate such an
undertaking? Surely none of us can be proud of the
moral and spiritual leadership which the institutional
church has given to the local communities these past
hundred years. Surely the church must accept its

full share of responsibility for the kind of world we
live in today.

Let us give the people the truth. Let them have
the facts. Their lives are filled with half-truths and
propaganda. Give them the facts, and we can depend
upon their judgment.

The job of the church is a teaching job, the job of
melting the ice in the hearts of men. Our minds are
frozen around a certain set of ideologies, around a
certain conceptual framework. In so many areas,
great groups and races of people have frozen in their
thinking. They refuse any longer to seek for a way
of understanding and brotherhood, but prefer, instead,
to maintain and perpetuate the same fears and anx-
ieties which have haunted them for generations. You
can see it constantly in the behavior of certain racial
and religious groups.

Yet there are still great areas in our American life
where minds are not frozen, where there is still hope,
where there is still time to build up positive philos-
ophies. But time is short, and immediate action is
necessary.

The institutional church cannot be proud of its performance in this field, for it, too, has accepted the
basic patterns of society. We have accepted patterns
which have tended to freeze the minds of people. We
cannot be proud as ministers and as a religious people
of the example we have set. We have accepted the
pattern of division, the pattern of separateness. Our
churches have become white collar organizations.

We have used the word "brotherhood," and to support that we have built tremendous missionary organizations to take the message of Christ to the far corners of the world. We have developed so many fine and handsome institutions of brick and mortar and stained glass, but what contribution have we made toward bridging the great gap of division and segregation at our community levels? Our evangelistic campaigns and world-wide missions are meaningless. We have preached Christ, but we have not practiced him. We have accepted the situation that members of our churches can be believers of the word and not doers of the word. And in doing it we have contributed to the moral breakdown and the moral dilemma of the world.

The great call of the church, the great religious revival, must take place in its leadership. The leaders must accept Christ, first, and do his bidding and give his word a positive philosophy in human relationships. Let the leadership do that, and the members will follow.

There are many across the country, Baptists and Presbyterians and Episcopalians and Methodists and Disciples, who have awakened to the real issues. There are many who are beginning to realize that they are responsible for much of the moral decadence of our time. They realize that the church has found an escape from economics and politics and social problems by claiming that these are not things vital to religion. And they have seen in their lifetime the fallacy of such a barren philosophy. It has been a lack of courage on their part that the world has not had a more positive approach to decency.

Religion is a part of all of life; it permeates the very being of people; it influences their attitudes and relationships, not only with regard to people, but also in relation to things. One of the strangest paradoxes of the present war and present crisis is that most of the leaders, the politicians, the economists, are people who are members of somebody's church and people who admit now with a good deal of shame the discrepancy between their apparent belief and their so-called pragmatic actions.

How then can the church make its contribution in the present crisis? The first responsibility is to begin with its own membership in the local community. The church must provide a new perspective, a new set of values. Its people must be able to see other people as potential friends rather than as enemies and competitors. We must face the basic role the church has played in the life of society and we must find a new interpretation of religious principles. The other responsibility is basically a teaching job. Men must learn to be decent; they must learn to want peace and to hate war, exploitation, and disease.

There are two great teaching vehicles in American life. There is the great public school system, where the intellectual lives of young people are developed and directed, where people give certain intellectual concepts to certain basic principles.

But perhaps the greatest educational vehicle in our society is the great school of the public, where people receive their early emotional and cultural conditioning: the family, play group, interest group, radio, press and news, where the mind-set of young children is fixed and where their attitudes are colored not only with regard to other people, but with regard to most of the things that they believe and feel. One of the great tasks which must be done in our society, at the community level, is to break down the barriers of communication and to break down the artificial walls, not only the legal walls which have been constructed in the courts in our basic attitudes of separateness, but also the informal and casual barriers which have grown up through custom and tradition which separate us. I know of no better place to start to build the Kingdom of God than in his church.

If people are to live in peace as nations, they must first learn to live in peace as neighbors. I realize that the church, perhaps, has gone as far as or farther than most of the so-called institutions in our communities. The minister, perhaps, is the most liberal, hard-working, and conscientious person there is. His heart, perhaps, bleeds at the sorrow, the hate, the exploitation, and the segregation. But the plain fact is the church has not been good enough to build the peace of the world. The truth still is that the bulk of the people who have made up our churches are no different in their basic attitudes in the whole field of human relations than the rest of the people who make up society.

The church must earn the right to leadership during this period. Of course, this is a difficult road.

Leadership has always been a sacrificial and difficult thing. Yes, we are pioneering. We are giving people new ideas, new values, a new sense of proportion. We are building in them now a sense of world community and of world fellowship. We have had the ideology for two thousand years, but the human co-efficient has prevented our making it work. For the first time we have the mechanisms in transportation and communication to visualize physically a unity which is the world.

We must create a new world attitude, a new conception of the peoples of the world. The present plans of world army and international organizations are but plans to postpone wars. They will not make peace. The people of the world must build a peaceful society which transcends national boundaries and isolationist ideologies. This is a job which cannot be done quickly. Culture is a thing which takes generations to develop. The job ahead is a long and difficult one, one which will require courage, patience, forbearance, determination, and great skill.

Not only must we be right and just in our claims for the church but we must also be exceedingly wise. Righteousness, justice, and wisdom are the great vehicles needed by the church to build a peace, a peace based on the brotherhood of man, the fatherhood of God. The universe was intended to function in an orderly fashion: one family, the human race, and one nation, the world.

We must toil unceasingly. Wherever there are people who have influence on others, whether they be politicians or businessmen, industrialists or labor leaders, we must seek them out and get across the gospel of unity and peace and brotherhood.

What if the church fails? you ask. This will not be the first time that a generation has failed its great challenge to build decency in the world. The cause of world peace, of world brotherhood, will not die. Institutionalized religion may die, but the Spirit of God will go on. For the people are ready and willing, if only the leaders will lead. I say we dare not fail!

Our chance has come to work and sweat and toil and suffer in the name of Jesus Christ, for the Kingdom of God beginning at home—in my town and in yours!

THE RACIAL ISSUE AND THE CHRISTIAN CHURCH

Georgia Harkness

THE race question might be described by Mark Twain's famous remark about the weather—it is the thing we talk most, and do least, about. As to what is the right and Christian thing to do, there is more agreement on racial issues than on war, economic change, or any other major social problem. The ground has been so many times gone over, usually with large agreement on general principles, that I have no hope of saying anything new in this address.

But when it comes to action, that is another matter! There is no point at which the practice of the church breaks sooner with its profession. For illustration, let us begin where we are. Neither this conference nor any other on "the church and the new world mind" could be held anywhere in the United States without first asking: "Will it be interracial? Where can we hold it safely?" Oxford and Delaware made far-reaching and profoundly Christian statements on race. But I have not known of many local churches where these affirmations have been discussed with full equality of Negro and white Christians in the group. Still more rare is the church or community where these affirmations have as yet radically altered practice.

The Madras Conference is generally conceded to have been the most democratic gathering, the most

186

fully representative of the world Christian community, that has been held in the history of the church. I for one can testify that its freedom from race consciousness and its living witness to the power of the Christian gospel to transcend all man-made distinctions is a continuing challenge. After Madras, teams of nationals were sent to various countries to interpret its meaning. Many of you will recall that in one of the teams that came to America was an African woman of great culture and spiritual power, Miss Minnie Soga. It is an index of our racial state that it was necessary to consider carefully to what communities Miss Soga could be sent.

The missionary enterprise can rightly be credited with having gone further than any other in the church in breaking down race prejudice. There is merited testimony by observers to the service of missionaries in creating "reservoirs of good will," and this service is not limited to the Orient. At the home front, thousands of local missionary societies have through the years been giving an education in world mindedness without which we should be far more parochial than we are. Yet no one needs to be told that church people have often been far more zealous for sending the Christian gospel to Africa than for being Christian toward the Negroes in their own community, for evangelizing Japan than for maintaining good will toward the Japanese in time of national conflict.

This disparity is so common that great numbers of us fall victim to it without recognizing it. To cite one or two illustrative instances, an able woman, well up in the leadership of the women's work of her denomination, made in my hearing an eloquent plea for racial equality in the church. I believe she meant all she said. Half an hour later at lunch, she told me she greatly preferred to have colored help in her home, for they knew how to keep their place! Last November after the Federal Council's Christian Mission on World Order, I was told about the meetings by a layman who had been greatly stirred. In the midst of an account of how the addresses had opened up the possibilities of a new world order was injected an indignant protest. A Negro soldier had jostled in the crowd this person whose soul had been so kindled by the vision of a new society! That such things can happen, not alone in the South but in any Northern community, gives witness by a continuing sequence of minor events to a major unhealed wound in the life of the church.

At every point in the race question we know what to do better than we do it. This discrepancy between knowledge and practice is our primary unsolved problem. But let us ask what lies back of it. Why is race prejudice such a pervasive human phenomenon?

CAUSES OF RACE PREJUDICE

Clearly it is not inborn. Colored and white children will play together, when permitted to do so, with full friendliness. Little Gentiles get along very well with little Jews, or at least as well as with other little Gentiles. It is when frightened parents erect

188

prohibitions that the seeds of prejudice are planted. These in most cases are planted early and grow luxuriantly.

Confront an adult with the fact of his race prejudice, and he will do one of three things. He will deny that he has it; he will admit it but admit also that it is irrational; or he will begin to rationalize his attitudes. The rationalizations usually take the form of words about inferior and superior races, about the danger of intermarriage, about dirt, smells, and cultural obnoxiousness, about treachery and "the yellow peril," about how those of other races "don't know their place" and are "creeping up on us." Conversation along these lines is so common that it must have a further word.

Race is a hard term to define because so many national, geographical, and linguistic factors are mixed up with it. As a matter of fact, though we sometimes speak of race in terms of the basic biological types, Caucasian, Mongolian, and Negroid, we are more apt to speak of Nordic, Anglo-Saxon, Teutonic, Slavic, Latin, Semitic, Scandinavian, Irish, European, Asiatic, African, Mexican, French Canadian, Japanese. Such adjectives indicate that what we really mean by race is not a pure biological stream, but what the Germans mean by *Volk*—a group sharing a common ethos and cultural tradition with some measure of national, geographical, and biological affinity. This looseness of diction in itself is evidence that race consciousness is far more a cultural than a biological thing. It precipitates the question of what, if anything, can be meant by superior and inferior races.

Race prejudice, though an ancient evil, received its intellectual formulation more recently than most of our evils. It was only ninety years ago that Count Gobineau published in French his four-volume *Essay on the Inequality of the Human Races,* in which he contended that color of skin determines mental and spiritual differences, and mixture of blood produces degeneracy and the fall of civilizations. This declaration, quoted and requoted in many forms, has done incalculable harm.

Anthropologists and psychologists have in recent years thoroughly exploded the superstitions to which Gobineau gave a pseudo-scientific foundation. In December, 1938, the American Psychological Association went on record declaring that there is no evidence of innate mental differences between races. The same year the American Anthropological Association asserted that there is no scientific basis for the biological inheritance of cultural traits, or of any traits implying racial inferiority.[1] So distinguished an anthropologist as Dr. Franz Boas writes in *Anthropology and Modern Life,* "If we were to select the most intelligent, imaginative, energetic and emotionally stable third of mankind, all races would be represented."[2] In the furor raised over the question of the Negro blood bank, medical science has corroborated the findings of anthropology and psychology by

---

[1]*Christian Bases of World Order,* pp. 104, 107.
[2]*Op. cit.,* p. 75.

declaring that there is no difference in the blood of colored and white persons, thus reinforcing the biblical word that God "hath made of one blood all nations of men" to dwell together.

Such scientific facts need to be recognized and popularized. Yet one does not need to be a scientist to see on how slender a thread the myth of biological racial superiority is suspended. For what, after all, is race? If it means color, there are fair Negroes and dark whites, swarthy Gentiles and blond, flaxen-haired Jews. If it means shape of skull, it is well to recall the Anglo-Saxon who, priding himself on his superiority because his head was long, discovered to his horror that two of his own children had long heads and the third a head that looked like a bullet slightly flattened on top. If it means facial contour, there are recognizable differences, but neither beauty nor ugliness is the exclusive possession of any race.

At the least suggestion of social equality and intercourse between the races the bogey of intermarriage lifts its head. Back of it lies a deep cultural cleavage, an ingrained dislike of the different, an irrational fear. I am not commending miscegenation, for I believe the Delaware Conference wisely wrote, "Assimilation of culture does not mean amalgamation of racial stocks." Yet intermarriage needs to be recognized for what it is, not a biological danger but a precipitation of cultural conflicts. Were these resolved, there would remain no reason why a person of any race should not marry a person of any other.

It is a combination of shortsightedness with cultural dissimilarity that lies at the root of our other rationalizations. Hasty generalization is rampant. If we say we dislike Negroes because they are ignorant and dirty, we fail, on the one hand, to recognize the great numbers who are not, and on the other, to confess our sin for having made them so. If we dislike Jews for being loudmouthed and scheming, a similar indictment holds, and we betray our forgetfulness of centuries of persecution which must generate self-assertion. If we dislike the Japanese and denounce their treachery, we forget that Pearl Harbor did not so much *create* as *reveal* deep-seated tensions in the Pacific Basin, to which the people of white nations have made no little contribution. It is difficult, but imperative, to keep our political judgments regarding Japan from being mixed up with a confused welter of emotional prejudice against the Japanese.

Ramifying through all these other factors are economic rivalry and a fear of loss of prestige and power by the influx of those of other racial stocks. This is evidenced by the fact that in industry, in schools, and in many aspects of community life a racial minority will be tolerated as long as it is *a very minor* minority. Let this minority increase, and barriers, both economic and social, are soon set up. Jews can attend most of our colleges until the proportion gets too high; then all sorts of subtle administrative devices are resorted to in order to keep down the number. We hear of Detroit race riots, but none in Des

Moines. This, if I may be pardoned for saying so, is not because Des Moines is inherently a more virtuous city! It is simply because there are more Negroes in Detroit and the industrial and housing tensions accordingly more acute.

What we have in the racial issue is a large-scale caste system, based primarily not on blood or economic function, but on misunderstanding of biological facts, lack of cultural appreciation, the mixture of political with racial ideologies, dislike of the different, rivalry, fear. This cultural cleavage has been ingrained through so many centuries of tradition that, although not innate, it is all but universal. Robert P. Tristam Coffin in a whimsical but nevertheless serious poem represents the men of Ur and Akkad as telling why they do not like each other.

The Man of Akkad:

> The men of Ur have heads too round.
> They have to build themselves a mound
> To reach their god. Their toes turn in,
> They have no hair upon their chin.
> They are not men. Their women wear
> The finer wool and build their hair
> High as towers in their pride,
> The men go meekly dressed in hide.
> They eat the fat part of their goats,
> Their speech is low down in their throats.
> To them the only proper word
> Is the thin edge of a sword.

The Man of Ur:

> The men of Akkad have no faces,
> Their curled beards are the nesting places
>   Of the vermin and the flea.
> They turn their toes out wantonly.
> Their heads are squeezed too long for brains,
> They have to ask their gods for rains.
>   They beat their wives, they wear soft clothes,
>   Their speech is high and through the nose,
> Their noses are as great as plows,
> They eat the udders of their cows.
>   The language that will suit them best
>   Is the arrow through the breast.

> Ur and Akkad are dead sands,
> But they have sons in living lands.[3]

So deep-rooted and therefore so unconscious are most of our antipathies that even Christian people find it harder to think dispassionately and act consistently on this subject than on any other. Racialism is the most deadly demon that infests our social structure and imperils the possibility of a free and democratic world.

EFFECTS

How does racialism imperil the peace of the world? Not *race,* which in the order of nature is ordained of God that there may be variety in the many families that make up the family of God, but *racialism.* Racialism is the perversion of this variety by the injec-

---

[3]Used by permission of the author.

tion of enmity, superiority, and contempt where there
ought to be fellowship in diversity. Since this is a
moral universe, racialism cannot go on without peril
to all—not to victor and victim, for there are no victors in this struggle—but to those who dominate and
those who suffer from the domination of others.

The effects of racialism go so deep and so nearly
encircle the globe that they can be mentioned only in
barest outline. Yet it is necessary to bring them
together if we are to see race prejudice for the pervasive and perilous thing it is.

To begin with Europe, there can be no other mood
than revulsion at the anti-Semitism of the Nazi regime, which in addition to untold agony for the living
is now estimated to have caused the death of three
million Jews. It is a reversion to barbarism in an
era which thought it had achieved some measure of
civilized culture. Yet it is a sword which cuts both
ways, and cuts deeper than the so-called "liquidation"
of the Jews, for there is enough racialism in all the
Allied nations to make the Nazi doctrine of race a
powerful interrogation. This has been stated succinctly by Carey McWilliams in *Brothers Under the
Skin:*

> The point to observe about Axis racial propa-
> ganda is the almost infinite possibilities or orien-
> tations which it can serve in this kind of war.
> It can be used to frighten the white population
> of this country; to arouse unrest among the Negro
> population; to embitter colored and mixed-breeds
> in Central and South America; to arouse distrust
> and suspicion among our colored allies; to mis-

lead the subject colored peoples of French Indo-China and the Dutch East Indies; to cause trouble between the United States and Great Britain; to stimulate Indian nationalistic ambitions and, at the same time, to make the fulfillment of these ambitions more difficult; to get the American people fighting among themselves over the Negro question and the entire Allied war ideology. . . . A more effective propaganda theme could not, in fact, have been devised. It is insidious, plausible, powerful, many-faceted, and inherently adaptable to multiple motivations.[4]

But Germany is not the only nation in Europe with a doctrine of race. To the east lies Russia, a country which though officially atheistic has actually achieved more racial equality than any other country in the world. While the Christian nations have been talking about the need of racial equality, under the Soviet regime it has become a fact. In Russia color of skin determines neither economic nor cultural opportunity. There is a speaking indictment in the fact that Paul Robeson took his family to Moscow so that his son could attend school in a country free from color restrictions.

Again, this situation presents a sword that cuts two ways. Let us rejoice heartily that there is race equality anywhere, whether under a Christian or Communist ideology. But let us beware. When the time comes to make the peace, the suppressed longings of the colored and racially underprivileged peoples of the world, if they do not see freedom in pros-

---

[4]Used by permission of Little, Brown & Co., publishers.

pect elsewhere, will turn to Russia to get it. The color question cannot fail to be a powerful leverage to enhance the authority of Russia after the war. One may doubt whether Russia is altruistic enough to use this authority to increase the welfare of the world; one cannot doubt that the union of capitalism with race discrimination puts a weapon of incalculable power in the hands of Mr. Stalin.

But what of the third great power in Europe? Great Britain has less race poison than Germany, less race equality than Russia. Can her mediating position establish peace?

Here a differentiation needs, of course, to be made between England and the Empire. With all its class distinction, England is more democratic than we are on the color question. In a recent study on "America and the Future," written by John K. Jessup, I find this interesting paragraph:

> The British can teach us much about racial tolerance. A British Negro was put out of a London hotel recently not because the hotel objected but because influential American guests did. England has no Chinese exclusion laws (although the dominions have). Nevertheless there is a dangerous and not altogether unreasoning Anglophobia in Asia which could, under certain conditions, align the Eastern races against all whites.[5]

In the last sentence lies dynamite. My own acquaintance with the Orient, consisting only of five

---

[5] Reprinted by courtesy of *Life* Magazine.

weeks in India at the time of the Madras Conference, is too limited to permit me to say anything authoritative. Yet one does not need to be in India five hours to discover the effects of empire and racial dominance in the souls of the people. In the faces and manner of the Indian masses, there is a patient and obsequious deference toward all "Europeans" (which includes Americans), but there is also a smoldering rebellion which flames easily under provocation. Much has been said of the disharmony among religious communities in India. There is one thing on which Hindu, Mohammedan, and Christian nationals of India are fully united—a passionate desire for freedom. The question of empire is, of course, not identical with that of color. Yet the two are so intertwined that there can be no peace for the world unless both are settled right. There are not a few in India who see no great choice to be made between British and Japanese domination, and who in the surging tide of color find more affinity with the other colored peoples of Asia than with Europeans.

Regarding China, I had better let one speak who has spent most of her life there and who knows the Chinese people intimately. Pearl Buck writes, in *What America Means to Me:*

> First and greatest of all our assets is the fact that we have the Chinese on the same side with us, because we are fighting Japan. We ought to make the most of the Chinese as our allies, because their very presence at our side cuts across

the dangerous division of Race. Have we made the most of China as an ally? No, certainly we have not.[6]

She then cites instances: the shipping of war materials to Japan, exclusion of Chinese from immigration and citizenship, refusal in Mississippi to allow Chinese children to go to school with white children, affronts to Chinese officials, other events of great military importance such as the meagerness of our shipment of supplies to China and the refusal of the British to let Chinese soldiers participate in the defense of Burma until it became apparent that the British could not hold out alone. She continues:

It is China alone who is contradicting by her very-presence at our side the Japanese propaganda that Britain and America will never cooperate with colored races. . . . She may be the one country some day which will prevent the war of East against West. But China needs reassurance and quick reassurance of her complete human equality in the mind of the white man.[7]

By the surrender of extraterritoriality rights in China and the belated passage of an act revoking Chinese exclusion, a step has been made toward such reassurance. Many more must be taken. With all their patience, I doubt whether the Chinese will readily forget that Hong Kong was long held by white power that has not yet promised to return it, and that for years in the International Settlement at

[6]Copyright, 1942, 1943, by Pearl S. Buck. The John Day Co., Inc., publisher. Used by special permission of the author's agent, David Lloyd.
[7]*Ibid.*

Shanghai, the only Chinese who could enter the parks were nursemaids caring for white children.

Coming to Japan, I shall not contend that racial tensions were the sole cause of the outbreak of war in the Pacific. But it is clear that the Oriental Exclusion Act, which abrogated our gentleman's agreement with Japan, has been a continuing insult since its passage in 1924. Furthermore, the story of what happened at Versailles, told by Paul Birdsall in *Versailles Twenty Years After* and retold by Paul Hutchinson in *From Victory to Peace,* ought to be equally well known. It was Baron Makino of Japan who tried to introduce into the Covenant of the League of Nations a statement affirming racial equality. This was blocked by Lord Robert Cecil for the British delegation, who said that it raised "extremely serious problems within the British Empire." Later Baron Makino reintroduced it in milder form, omitting the dangerous word "race" and asking only to have inserted in the preamble of the covenant the innocuous words, "by the endorsement of the principles of the equality of nations and just treatment of their nationals." This, too, was opposed by British and American representatives on the score that it would interfere with the sovereignty of states and would raise the race issue throughout the world. The amendment was lost. In its failure is epitomized much of the failure of the League to hold the world together, and much of the reason why the East does not trust the pretensions of Western nations to democracy.

Of an impending war of East against West a generation hence, a third world war in which the colored peoples who constitute two-thirds of the world's population would be arrayed against the one-third who are white, I have not the political wisdom to speak. Yet it requires no great knowledge of political science to observe dark clouds in the sky. It is ominous that neither in the Cairo agreement nor in any other declaration of the United Nations has a statement been made regarding the disposition of the territories seized by Japan in 1941. If they are to be returned to their former possessors under terms that permit exploitation by white business interests, the resulting tensions will head toward another global war. The colored peoples of the earth will not consent indefinitely to be denied the fruit of their land and labor. The slogan, "Asia for the Asiatics" is a powerful weapon, not simply because it is wielded by a strong nation now our enemy, but because it expresses the latent animosities and hopes of a vast colored continent. That these peoples should remain our friends is of incalculable importance to the future peace of the world. There is little hope that they will remain our friends and allies unless the race demon is mastered and we learn to treat them as friends and equals.

There is no time to speak of South Africa, where the racial pretensions that first aroused Mr. Gandhi to action forty years ago have not moderated. Paul Hutchinson says of them, "As to the racial laws in South Africa, and the white opinion which insists upon them and sees that they are enforced, one can only say that they are probably preparing the way for the most tragic racial conflict that the world has ever seen."[8] Nor is there time to speak of South America, where the tensions, though less severe, are a simmering mass ready to boil up whenever heat is applied.

Nor is there time to speak in any detail of the effects of race prejudice in our own country. We are familiar with them. The Delaware Conference put it as succinctly as I have found it anywhere: "In our own country millions of people, especially American Negroes, are subjected to discrimination and unequal treatment in educational opportunities, in employment, wages and conditions of work, in access to professional and business opportunities, in housing, in transportation, in the administration of justice and even in the right to vote."

Back of these fifty words lies an incalculable amount of human misery, frustration, the embarrassment of never knowing when one may be publicly rebuffed, the necessity of seeing one's children denied what is accorded to white children as their natural birthright. When a race riot breaks out in Los Angeles, Detroit, or Harlem, it is a spectacular event that makes the headlines. Back of every such outburst lie a multitude of unpublicized acts and attitudes of racial snobbery which are un-Christian, undemocratic, and, in the truest sense, un-American.

---

[8]*From Victory to Peace*, by Paul Hutchinson, p. 110. Used by permission of Willett, Clark & Co., publishers.

It is not surprising that as we fight a war to save democracy, Negro Americans and Japanese Americans, segregated even in the very process of fighting for their country, should ask the pointed question, "What democracy?" As I heard it put recently by an impassioned Negro minister, "When our boys get to Europe or the Solomons are the bullets going to come marked 'For Whites Only'?" The surprising thing is not that there should be outcroppings of bitterness and even riots, but that there should be as few of them as there are. Were the tables turned, could the white people of this country show as much cooperation and restraint?

The internment of 110,000 Japanese on the Pacific Coast, including more than 70,000 American citizens, will, I am sure, long remain a blot upon our democracy. It is a sobering fact that as war encircles the globe, Germany is the only country outside of the United States that has thought it necessary to intern any considerable number of its own citizens. I do not say that the treatment accorded to the Japanese in the relocation centers is comparable to the German concentration camp. Yet in the loss of economic security and professional opportunity, the uprooting of families and surrender of personal liberty, that have been forced upon great numbers of our fellow citizens and loyal neighbors, there is something of which no American can be proud. One wonders whether, in the history books of the future, we shall try as hard to forget it as we now do the Mexican War.

The Church

But our subject is, "The Racial Issue and the Christian Church." If the things I have stated are facts, the church cannot let these conditions continue without action. The security of the world calls for the mitigation of racial tensions by the doing of justice. Deeper than the demand for security is the obligation of the Christian gospel to increase love.

In the first place, the church must understand and proclaim its gospel. Vague generalities about the fatherhood of God and the brotherhood, of man have often been spoken which do not cut down through our crust of convention to where the race problem is. We need to recover the insights of Jesus on this question. And one of the most amazing things about Jesus is how he met the racialism of his day. Reared in a Jewish tradition that prided itself on being the chosen people of God, living in occupied territory where Roman superiority and Jewish superiority were always in uneasy tension, he lived on a plane that made even a Roman centurion say of him, "Truly this man was the Son of God." Jew, Roman, Samaritan, Syro-Phenician were to him equally the children of God. In the presence of human need, his healing knew no bounds.

If we examine the democracy of Jesus—a democracy which he never talked about but always practiced —certain dominant traits appear. It was based on a living conviction of man's relation to God. This relation was one of love which called forth obligations to God and man, and one finds in Jesus not an injunc-

204

tion to the claiming of rights but to the doing of duties. It was linked with a realistic view of human nature, for "he knew what was in man" and saw in man both sin and supreme greatness. Concern for all persons was expressed naturally and without pretension in the acts and attitudes of daily life. These four—divine dependence, mutual obligation stemming from love, sound judgment of human nature, and the practice of brotherhood in daily experience—are the basis of any true democracy. Not until the church both preaches and practices such Christian democracy will it touch the fringes of the race question.

Second, the church must put its own house in order. This means the welcome presence of colored Christians in the worship services, church schools, discussion groups, and social gatherings of the church. It means the presence of colored persons in the conferences and policy-making bodies of the Church. It means the refusal to permit segregation in the living arrangements connected with church meetings. It means the sharing of the recreational, educational, and hospital facilities of the church with all who need them. It means the interchange of pulpits between colored and white ministers. It means equal pay for the colored and white servants of the church. If such a program arouses opposition, it means the tactful but courageous insistence that the house of God is a place of prayer and of service for all peoples.

I am aware that the relatively mild proposals of the preceding sentences, if acted upon, would be revolutionary. Already I hear someone say, "You couldn't do that in my community!" Have you tried? The ideal of race equality will not arrive all at once. But it will not arrive at all until we stop conforming to the prevailing mores and give the church an opportunity to lead in the shaping of community standards. Even conflict, if dealt with in love, can prove a creative experience.

Third, the church must lift its voice and use its influence for the curbing of racialism outside its own walls. Its most necessary service is the re-education of its members to greater sensitiveness in personal relations. The implications of the Christian gospel when applied to daily life must be pointed out. Education as to the cultural achievements and contributions of those of other races is imperative. There must be sympathetic interpretation both of colored to white and of white to colored, for fellowship can exist only as a two-way process.

The race problem must, for the most part, be met by person-to-person contacts which create understanding. This calls for more intervisitation and social fellowship, both locally and nationally, and, as occasion permits, in the world community. It is hard to remain hostile toward a people whose individuals one has come to know and love.

In cases of racial discrimination by public agencies within the community, the church must be willing to stand up and be counted on the side of equality. It must act in cooperation with other community forces if possible, but in any case, it must act. Not alone prophetic indictment, but patient mediation, is the function of Christian leaders.

From time to time, political aspects of the question call for legislative action. The Oriental Exclusion Act, still only partially removed, is a case in point, as is the poll tax issue. Many complex aspects of foreign and domestic policy will demand action. In such matters the church must throw the searchlight of the gospel on the question and help its members to act, as citizens, in the light of a Christian decision.

Finally, the total problem must be lifted into the realm of prayer and worship. We must pray for those of other races; we must be responsive to the awareness that they are praying for us. When one enters truly into the mood of intercession, bitterness departs, and fellowship takes its place. And if it is God's business we are engaged in, we must give God an opening in our souls.

In the midst of the difficulties, the walls of opposition, the heartaches, the dim clouds of uncertainty that surround the question, let us not despair. God lives; we are not alone. He has sent his Son in love to break down the middle walls of partition that we in our pride and selfishness have erected. In his name and spirit let us pray, "Thy Kingdom come; Thy will be done on earth." And in his name and spirit, let us go forward to do it.

HOW CAN THE CHURCHES IN AMERICA WORK FOR PEACE?

WALTER W. VAN KIRK

NO MORE important issue confronts the churches of America than the establishment and maintenance of world order. Without world order the Kingdom of God on earth will remain an abstraction of theological speculation. Without world order there will be such an enlargement of military establishments with such a resulting drain upon the physical wealth of all peoples as will endanger not only the material but the spiritual health of the world of nations. It is not a question of guns or butter. If that were all, we could probably do without butter. It is a question of guns or schools, guns or churches, guns or freedom of speech, guns or freedom of religion. If we do not have world order we shall have world regimentation. If we have world regimentation, there will be little opportunity for the free exercise of the gifts of the spirit. How, then, can the churches of America work for world justice and peace?

In the first place, the churches of America must have an informed mind. Speaking generally, the churches do not have an informed mind on world problems. This statement may be challenged in view of the many affirmations on war and peace adopted by our various religious assemblies. Placed one on top of the other these resolutions, figuratively speaking, would reach to the ceiling or beyond. In a sense, that is the fatal weakness of these resolutions. They are too often pyramided on a vertical line, whereas they should be spread abroad on a horizontal plane. For many of our people the ideas embodied in these affirmations remain in the "stratosphere" of ecclesiastical verbiage. The time has come to bring these ideas down to earth where people earn their bread and butter, where people vote, and where people fight and die. The resolutions of the churches on peace and international order have been useful in orienting the Christian community to the task of creating a warless world. They have, to a degree, been helpful in the shaping of public opinion. But the ease with which many of our churchmen adopt resolutions with scarcely a thought as to how these affirmations may be integrated in the total program of Christian education is disquieting, to say the least.

It is clear, therefore, that our churches must do more than pass resolutions. They must make the quest for world order a priority concern. There are hopeful signs that Christians are getting ready to do this. In November of last year many denominations cooperated in taking the Christian Mission on World Order to 100 American cities. The Methodists have just concluded their "Bishops' Crusade" for the winning of the peace. This conference of the Disciples of Christ is a step in the right direction. Scores of local churches are promoting institutes and study conferences on world order. In England, Canada, New Zealand, and Australia, efforts are under way to help Christians understand how imperative it is that a righteous peace be established after today's bloodletting is over. In

China, the National Christian Council is launching an educational campaign in the interest of a just and durable peace. The World Council of Churches, with its headquarters in Geneva, is probing the minds of Christians in many lands with respect to postwar problems.

But the peace movement within the American churches is still regarded by the vast numbers of our people as an "extra," and as an "extra" it is treated as a foundling by the holders of ecclesiastical purse strings. Taken together, our various denominations pour millions of dollars into home missions and foreign missions. They donate still more millions to feeding and clothing the victims of war and to rebuilding their destroyed churches and cathedrals. But when it comes to securing sizable appropriations from official church treasuries to promote a program of peace education and action among Christians—well, that is something else. That is an "extra," and as such it is not believed to have a claim upon the resources of the church comparable to the more orthodox claims of home and foreign missions and church extension.

The gifts of Christian generosity invested in the missionary enterprise are, of course, an investment in peace. In many respects our missionaries occupy advance positions in the struggle for international decency and world order. The discontent reflected in the purpose of unnumbered millions in colonial lands and subject territories to achieve for themselves political freedom and economic justice is a divine discontent

210

derived, in part, from the gospel story proclaimed by missionary ambassadors of our Lord. So, too, the money expended on Christian education may be said to represent an investment in peace.

Even so, there is still lacking in many of our communions a conscious purpose to orient missionary and Christian education activities to the task of achieving world order. Too many individual Christians who lay their gifts upon the altar to evangelize the world for Christ do not feel themselves to be a part of the movement to reorganize the structure of international society in the interest of peace. This is due to the fact that our denominations, in the main, look upon their over-all activities as not being related to the quest for world order.

Fortunately this picture is not wholly black. Modest grants are made available to the peace commissions and committees of a few of our communions. But the monies directly expended by our churches looking toward the uprooting of war, and the establishment of international justice and good will, are pitiably small when contrasted with the total giving of our churches for other concerns. If you do not believe this, take a look at the national headquarters of our denominations. You will see there innumerable offices, each staffed with an able secretariat, and each supported by adequate funds, so that natives in the Solomon Islands may be converted to Christ, or that struggling churches on the home front may be perpetuated, or that ministers may be insured an adequate retirement allowance, or that men's work and women's work and children's work may be advanced, or that church records may be kept in order. But the responsibility of galvanizing our churches into action to the end that their peace resolutions may be more widely studied and understood and their prayers for peace may be heard in the White House and in the halls of Congress is often left to the part-time labors of a single executive who is already overburdened with a thousand and one other duties. The center of gravity of denominational activity must now be directed to the total task of ridding the world of the vice of war.

This issue of world order is a "must." It is a "must" for which Christ died. The preparation of the Christian mind in an understanding of the political, economic, moral, and cultural requirements of world order is also a "must." If we do not solve the problem of war, if we are impotent as Christians in the shaping of the peace, we shall build new churches in Europe, China, Africa, and elsewhere only to have these churches destroyed when once again the fury of war is loosed upon the earth. Until world order is achieved we shall send missionaries to distant places only to have these missionaries returned on some future "Gripsholm" when once again the swords of wrath are drawn. During the past two years many of our communions have raised vast sums for war relief. This is splendid. This is what Christ would have us do. But how long shall we be content to raise money to buy food and clothing for the victims of war while at the same time failing to make a frontal attack upon war itself? Millions of dollars for war relief. But only small change for peace education and peace action.

This business of uprooting war and of laying the foundations of an enduring peace is not a part-time job. This is not something that can be accomplished upon a penny basis. This is a task that requires the constant and untiring efforts of our churches in the preparation of educational materials, in the fostering of discussion groups, in the mobilization of Christian opinion and the reflection of that opinion in political conduct, in the orientation of the total life of our churches to the sheathing of the sword and in making crystal clear the relation of the gospel of our Risen Lord to the establishment of economic and political justice among and between the nations. Before the churches in America can effectively work for peace they must be prepared to provide the funds and the personnel required to transform their peace resolutions into a flaming and dynamic evangel.

Toward this end, each denomination should discontinue the policy of peace by pennies and appropriate for the explicit purpose of peace education a considerably larger fraction of its total income. Each denomination, where this has not already been done, should create a department or a commission charged with the responsibility of promoting a program of peace action. Each of these denominational departments or commissions should be related to the Federal Council of the Churches of Christ in America, the International Council of Religious Education, the Foreign Missions

Conference, and the Home Missions Council, so that
there may be developed an over-all, nation-wide strategy of the churches in their pursuit of peace. In certain respects the Federal Council's Commission on a
Just and Durable Peace may be said to be developing
just such a strategy. But this commission is hampered
by the fact that too few of our denominations feel any
sense of direct responsibility for the shaping of its
program or for the meeting of its financial needs.
Each of the larger communions might well make available to the Commission on a Just and Durable Peace
one full-time executive whose sole responsibility would
be that of interpreting the policies of the commission
to his own constituency. Before it can be said that
the churches are working in dead earnest for peace,
there must be more adequate personnel, more money,
more planning by national headquarters, more and
better educational materials, more study conferences
and institutes, more preachers and church school
teachers competent to discuss the fundamental requirements of world order. Then and not until then will our
peace resolutions come within the intellectual grasp
of the great masses of Christian thinking people.

In the second place, our American churches can
work for peace by exercising vigilance with respect to
current international developments. It seems clear
now that the peace will not be made at a conference
convened by the victors at the end of the war. We
shall not have another Paris Peace Conference nor
another Treaty of Versailles. The peace is being made
coincident with the waging of the war. As proof of

this we have only to look at the Atlantic Charter, the
agreements for the liquidation of Lend-Lease, the Moscow Conference, the Cairo Conference, the Teheran
Conference, the creation of a European Advisory Committee to examine European questions as the war develops and the peace approaches, the establishment of
a Special Advisory Council for matters relating to
Italy, the creation of the United Nations Relief and
Rehabilitation Administration, and the current negotiations with respect to the Russian-Polish border.

So accustomed are we to thinking in terms of a
formal peace conference such as that convened in
Paris at the close of the first world war that these
current developments are not given the attention they
deserve. It is rather naïvely assumed by some of our
people that there will be plenty of time to mobilize
Christian support for world order once the anticipated
peace conference gets under way. It is proposed, for
example, that an outstanding Christian be deputized
to sit at the conference and in this way bring the influence of Christian thought to bear upon the winning
of the peace. This is but typical of the short-cut
method by which Christians are all too prone to effect
social reform. We want to do the unusual, the spectacular. We want to beat the drums of denominational
drama and put a churchman on display at a peace conference on the assumption, I suppose, that a man
dressed in clerics will be able by his presence to transform politicians into peacemakers.

It is silly to expect that a representative of the
churches at a postwar peace conference will be able to

exercise a kind of magic restraint on diplomats who might otherwise repeat the blunders of the statesmanship of former days. No amount of ecclesiastical showmanship in the presence of clicking cameras can take the place of the less dramatic but infinitely more rewarding procedure of stimulating an intelligent interest in the minds of millions of Christians with respect to the day-by-day decisions upon which even now the nature of the peace is being determined. If the spokesmen of governments are to lay aside the instruments of power politics it will not be because there is a representative of the churches at a future peace conference but because the churches are able to develop meanwhile a sound and persuasive public opinion in support of policies of international collaboration. That is why it is so important that the American churches study the political developments previously referred to with the view to interpreting these developments in the light of Christian principles.

If these day-by-day negotiations looking toward the peace are consonant with Christian principles, let the people of our churches say so and support the government in the enunciation of these policies. If, on the other hand, these current developments are at variance with Christian principles, let the people of our churches say so and advise our government leaders accordingly. For example, the Moscow Conference, in its insistence upon a general international organization, seemed to meet the requirements for world order laid down in the first of the Six Pillars of Peace approved by the Federal Council. The Moscow Declaration pledges that "united action . . . will be continued for the organization and maintenance of peace and security" and recognizes "the necessity of establishing at the earliest practicable date, a general international organization, based on the principle of the sovereign equality of all peace-loving States, and open to membership by all such States." This affirmation comes pretty close to paralleling the recommendation of the Delaware Conference (1942) "that the United States pursue a responsible national policy with concern for the welfare of all peoples and that the United States cooperate fully with all nations and peoples in working towards a world order of justice and peace." It would be interesting to discover how many of the delegates to the Delaware Conference, or how many of our Christian people generally, took the time or the trouble to write to the President or to the Secretary of State or to their respective congressmen or senators approving this part of the Moscow Declaration.

The Cairo Conference, on the other hand, laid down a policy with respect to Japan that carries with it the seeds of future war. In the Cairo communiqué, Japan was to be stripped of her territorial gains acquired by military aggression, which all will agree is in the interest of justice. But no assurance was forthcoming that Japan, stripped of her stolen territory and delivered from the bondage of her war lords, was to be accorded the right of economic intercourse with other nations. No promise was forthcoming that the Japanese people were to be given the opportunity to earn a legitimate livelihood, despite the assurance of the Atlantic Char-

ter that all states, victors as well as vanquished, shall
be provided access "on equal terms, to the trade and
raw materials of the world which are needed for their
economic prosperity." Nor was anything said at
Cairo regarding the restoration of Hong Kong to
China. Nothing was said at Cairo regarding the possible independence of the territories in the East Indies
and Southwest Asia hitherto occupied by Japan and
from which areas that country is to be forcibly ejected.
If the Cairo Declaration is to be regarded as the last
word on East Asia, a third world war is already in the
making. Again, it would be interesting to discover
how many of our Christian people took the time or the
trouble to make known their disapproval of the Cairo
communiqué to our leaders in Washington.

Or take the recent debates on foreign policy in the
Congress of the United States. In the House, the Ful-
bright Resolution, and in the Senate, the Connally Resolution, both of which pledged this country to policies
of postwar collaboration, were adopted by substantial
majorities. It would be interesting to discover how
many of our Christian people exercised their rights as
citizens in a democracy by making known their views
on this issue to their representatives in Washington.
For many years the churches have condemned the
practice and policy of American isolation. The Congress has now indicated its purpose to abandon isolation and to pursue henceforth a policy of collaboration
with other nations for the maintenance of peace. In
this decision the Congress has acted in accordance with
the expressed will of the people of our churches. Had

only a small fraction of our people written to their congressmen supporting this action, a public opinion would thereby have been engendered looking toward the day when the Congress will be called upon to implement these resolutions.

Again, take this matter of feeding the starving people of Europe. There is pending in the Senate, at this very moment, a bill advising the President and the Secretary of State that it is the sense of the Senate that a way be found to feed the starving babies and the undernourished parents in Nazi-occupied countries. Unless these people are fed, and fed quickly, they will die, and in dying, they will engender among those who survive, such a mood of hostility and of hatred as will make infinitely more difficult the achieving of peace throughout the continent of Europe. We are asking our people to contribute relief funds so that when the war is over, the hungry may be fed, and the naked may be clothed. Meanwhile, unless action is taken quickly, thousands of these intended beneficiaries of our generosity will die. It would be interesting to discover how many of our Christian thinking people even know that such a bill is pending in the Senate and to discover how many of those possessed of this knowledge are doing anything at all to insure its passage by the Senate. What is the value of Christians adopting affirmations on world order, to be achieved in some indefinite future, if at this moment of desperate need, we do not do more than we have yet done to make certain that the Europe of tomorrow will be something more than a graveyard?

We see here one of the most glaring defects in the strategy of our American churches in their quest for a righteous peace. We resolve and we preach and we pray, but we are too often passive and inarticulate at the precise moment when we should be speaking either for or against measures by the Congress that conform to or are in violation of the principles to which we are committed. The foreign policy of the United States is not decided in our denominational assemblies. The foreign policy of this country is decided by the American Congress and more particularly by the Senate. The churches, accordingly, can work for peace and world order by urging Christians, through intelligent political action, to take a more responsible part in the shaping of American foreign policy. It is not proposed that Christians march on Washington and engage in high-pressure lobbying that smacks of ecclesiastical authoritarianism. This is a form of political activity repugnant to the Protestant tradition. Nor is it proposed that our pulpits be used for the dissemination of partisan political propaganda. It is proposed, however, that Christians, as citizens, make known to Congress the consensus of American Christian opinion with respect to our national political conduct.

And this would seem to be the place for a word of caution and for the exposition of a dilemma with which we may be confronted after the war. American Christians have set high standards by which the world of tomorrow is to be judged. So, too, have the Christians of other countries. The Six Pillars of Peace put forth by the Federal Council's Commission anticipate the creation of an international society that may not be achieved as quickly as some of us might desire. Time will be required to liquidate age-old injustices, and still more time will be required to uproot the vice of power politics and to establish in the place of military alliances a world system of law and order. It is the right and duty of Christians to insist that nations shall act in accordance with the precepts of the New Testament gospel. Those are absolutes of international conduct to which Christians must be forever bound. But the world of nations is not Christian. Taking into account the population of the entire globe, Christians are a minority people. And within this minority, vast numbers are not yet convinced of the relevancy of the gospel to the political and economic conduct of nations. Even among people nominally espousing the Christian ethic, there is a pervasive reliance upon the instruments of physical power.

How, then, can it be expected that the postwar world shall be organized wholly within the pattern of Christian absolutes? It is neither reasonable nor practicable to expect that this shall be done. The likelihood is that the peace will be both a good peace and a bad peace. In view of this fact, we must fortify ourselves in advance against the disillusionment that might otherwise possess us when boundary lines are drawn, not by the precision instruments of Christian perception, but by the pen points of political power. If we desire freedom and justice for subject peoples and that freedom and justice are not reasonably secured when the war is over, what shall we, as Christians, do? Suppose, instead of the all-inclusive world organization for which Christians pray, there is established after the war a coalition of victor powers. What then shall we, as Christians, do?

The answers to these questions are likely to involve for all of us, as Christians and as citizens, a most painful experience. If, on the one hand, we oppose the settlement on the ground that Christian principles have been compromised, we shall be driven into the illogical position of supporting American isolation, despite the fact that we recognize isolation to be essentially pagan in its conception and in its practice. Moreover, if by reason of the opposition of Christian forces, the United States withdraws from a peace that is the by-product of power politics, have we not unhappily catapulted our country into the vortex of the very system of power politics against which we protest, since, if America withdraws from the peace, we shall have, not one, but two systems of power politics? Again, if as Christians we are not wholly satisfied with the peace and if for this reason we counsel and make certain America's abstention from the postwar world, are we not thereby withdrawing the influence of the one nation that might most reasonably be expected to influence for the good an otherwise bad peace? Also, will not such a decision on our part, a decision motivated by considerations of high principle, have the effect of throwing Christians into political comradeship with those blatant patrioteers and jingoistic nationalists and self-seeking interest groups that long for the fleshpots of normalcy?

If, on the other hand, we who hold that Christian ideals are relevant to the world of nations, support a bad peace, will it not be said that we have betrayed our Lord and compromised our ideals? If, in such circumstances, we, as Christians, advise and make certain American collaboration in a system of power politics and of military alliances, have we not thereby put out of the reach of subject peoples the one nation to which they might otherwise appeal in the hour of their greatest need? If Christians support a peace that falls short of their own definition of the minimum requirements of justice, will not such support engender in the minds of the secular community a profound contempt for the moral preachments of the Christian community? If we, as Christians, give assent to a peace that is hardly more than a compromise between competing imperialistic interests, will not the churches forfeit the right to be regarded as God's mouthpiece in the wilderness of this modern world?

I propound these questions but I do not have the answers. Events which cannot now be foreseen will determine in large part the answers that must some day be given. Perhaps it is enough at this moment to do two things: first, to bring the maximum of Christian influence to bear upon our government, so that the peace may more nearly approximate the ideals set forth by the churches than now seems likely; and, second, to advise the people of our churches that if the kind of peace to which they are committed is neither achieved in fact nor anticipated in theory, the political action of Christians will have to be determined in the light of the then existing situation.

In the third place, our American churches can work for peace by accelerating the movement for inter-church cooperation and Christian unity. A disunited Church is at a serious disadvantage when it proclaims the need for a united world. The secular community is entirely within its right when it says to the churches: "Physician, heal thyself." If it is true that a mistaken conception of national sovereignty has bedeviled the relations of nations, it is no less true that a mistaken conception of denominational sovereignty has bedeviled the relations of churches.

In that area of Europe commonly known as "the Balkans," there is a grouping of small nations, each preoccupied with its own sovereign rights, each zealous for the protection of its own boundaries, each determined to preserve without compromise its historic heritage. For too long a time the churches have been "Balkanized." Even now, despite the progress achieved in the direction of interdenominational cooperation and Christian unity, the average American community, in its religious organization, represents an ecclesiastical counterpart of "the Balkans." In many towns of 500 to 5,000 people, there are several churches of differing communions, each within a stone's throw of the others. I am thinking of one such community with which I am personally familiar. It is a town of 800 people. In this town there are five churches. Three of them are varieties of the Presbyterian church, one is a Methodist church, and one a Disciples of Christ church. Within a five-minute period, one can walk past the doors of all of these churches. Each of these five churches is struggling to keep its roof in repair. There are five preachers, five janitors, five ecclesiastical overheads whose financial requirements must be met. And yet, in this town there is no community center for young people, none except the village saloon. Were these churches to unite, they could immensely enrich their service of worship, and the money now spent to maintain five churches and five preachers and five janitors and five ecclesiastical overheads could be used in part to provide the youth of that village with opportunities for wholesome and character-building recreation. The situation I have just described could be paralleled in thousands of communities throughout the United States. Considering the fact that these churches recognize in Jesus Christ a common sovereignty to which they are in conscience bound, it might well be asked: Why must this disunity be suffered to continue? If the smaller states of Europe are to be asked to make concessions in the interest of European solidarity, is it any less reasonable to anticipate that the churches of America shall make concessions in the interest of spiritual solidarity? If all the nations, large and small, are to be asked to yield certain of their sovereign rights to the international community for the sake of world order, is it any less reasonable to anticipate that all churches, large and small, in our own and other countries, shall yield cer-

tain of their denominational rights in the achievement
of a church that will truly reflect the oneness of Christian believers?

We may well rejoice in the fact that through the
Federal Council of the Churches and kindred bodies,
many of the larger and more influential communions
in the United States are practicing the principle of cooperation. We may well rejoice in the fact that in the
World Council of Churches we see, however dimly, the
outline of the ecumenical church. But in these inter-
church movements there has been little if any renun-
ciation of the prerogatives of ecclesiastical sovereignty. The time has now come when the churches
must with greater boldness and daring greatly expand
the areas of interchurch cooperation. If in the interest
of world order, the economic practices of the nations
are to be modified and oriented to the requirements of
the international community, why should not the economic practices of our several denominations be oriented to the total needs of the Kingdom without regard to denominational considerations? If, in the interest of world order, the armies and navies and air
forces of the nations are to be pooled for the preservation of peace, why should not the leadership and resources of our churches be pooled for the evangeliza-
tion of the world?

My impression is that the secular community is
thoroughly impatient with churches which continually
call upon the nations to engage in a great and solemn
act of self-renunciation for the purpose of putting an
end to the anarchy resulting from competing national-

isms, while, at the same time, these same churches, or
many of them, refuse to engage in similar acts of re-
nunciation for the purpose of putting an end to the
anarchy resulting from our competing sectarianism.
I can think of nothing that would so inspire the plain
people of all lands to make whatever sacrifices may be
required to establish a world community than for
Christians to support a great forward movement of
church cooperation and Christian unity among the
various communions of our own and other countries.

The skepticism of the secular community with respect to the churches does not derive from doubts regarding the validity of creedal affirmations but rather
from doubts regarding the willingness of the churches
to practice among themselves the principles of cooperation and unity which they proclaim for the nations.
The United States census of 1936 showed that there
are in this country 256 denominations. This is a situation of extreme gravity. We are living in a dynamic
and revolutionary age, an age in which the quest for
cultural and political solidarity has become the con-
suming passion of statesmen and scientists, poets and
philosophers. And the best the churches can do in
matching the opportunities of this revolutionary hour
is to offer the American public 256 varieties of religious organization, the great majority of which had
their inception under circumstances wholly unrelated
to the precedent-smashing events of the days in which
we live! We cannot pour the new wine of tomorrow's
world into the old ecclesiastical wineskins. The fer-
ment of social change bids fair to alter the industrial,

political, and cultural framework of the civilization inherited from our fathers. The call is for a spiritual
reformation in which the structural disunity of Protestantism shall be superseded by such a sacrificial striv-
ing for unity as will convince an otherwise skeptical
public that the churches are prepared to practice what
they preach. What we do in this respect will more
surely advance the cause of world order than what we
say in the resolutions on world justice and peace
adopted by our church assemblies.

In the fourth place, our American churches can work
for peace by constantly emphasizing the futility and
hopelessness of a postwar settlement dictated by considerations of hatred and revenge. Nobody will deny
that there is today a vast amount of hatred abroad
in the world. This is understandable. Without accepting as literally true all the atrocity stories head-
lined in our daily press, it is a matter of common
knowledge that millions of people have suffered cruel-
ties and deprivations unparalleled in history. Racial
minorities have been beaten and driven from their
homes. Whole populations in occupied countries have
been denied those freedoms without which life is a
living death. Secret police have intimidated and
physically assaulted those who refused to bend their
knees to man-made gods. From concentration camps,
there has arisen the pained cry of the tortured. Hus-
bands have been separated from their wives and parents from their children. Patriots dangle from the
hangman's noose. Hunger stalks through Europe.
Millions of able-bodied men are deported to Germany

to make bullets with which their own flesh and blood may be killed. It is natural to hate under these circumstances. Nor is it for us to sit in judgment on those who nurture thoughts of revenge and retaliation.

While in England some months ago, I was told a story that frightened me. An Anglican bishop informed me that preparations are under way in the Lowlands and in Norway for the celebration of "Hatchet Day." You cannot buy a hatchet in any of these countries, and the reason for this is simple enough. It was explained to me that the names of the "Quislings" and the functionaries of the Nazis are catalogued and filed away in anticipation of the day when hatchets will swing and heads will roll. There is enough hatred resident in the hearts and minds of men today to make whatever may be left of our civilization a wilderness of anarchy and debauchery. Whether or not this mass hatred can be held in leash long enough to enable the postwar forces of law and order to prevail is an open question. Certainly this cannot be done if the churches yield to the temptation to substitute for the Christian gospel of reconciliation the pagan doctrine of retaliation.

Here is an area in which the churches may speak without fear of trespassing upon the functions of the state. Nor have we any choice in this matter. We are under the compulsion of a God-given mandate when we cry out against the ravages of a blind and unreasoning hate. But are we crying out? In our resolutions, yes. And, within limits, by our action, too. Many of our communions and interchurch bodies, in our own

229

and in other countries, have warned against the sin and the peril of hating. In many areas of this "blackout" world, it is the voice of Christendom that has given hope to persecuted racial and religious minorities.

Despite this fact it cannot be said that our churches, in their community relations, have been sufficiently articulate in their protestations against the rising tides of hatred in our own country. When popular magazine writers and radio commentators tell us that hatred of the enemy is a necessary weapon of war, every pulpit in America should resound with a denunciation of this pagan thesis. When military officers tell us that without hatred soldiers cannot be soldiers, every pulpit in America should hold up such utterances to public scorn.

In theory our churches denounce the mistreatment of Japanese minorities within our midst. But not often enough are these same churches prepared to risk the displeasure of the local community by seeking employment and decent housing facilities for those Japanese Americans whose patriotism is vouched for by the FBI and by the War Relocation Authority. Jesus Christ is crucified afresh every time a minister of the gospel remains silent in the presence of those who advocate hating our enemies. Nails are once more driven into the body of our Lord every time a minister or the members of his congregation remain mute when on the motion picture screen or by the public press, Germans or Japanese are depicted as animals belonging to a subhuman order of creation.

Every time a synagogue has scribbled upon it the sign of the swastika or the Jews in your neighborhood and mine are subjected to the abuses of an un-American hoodlumism and there is not instantly forthcoming from the clergy and laity of the community a demand that such abuses be stopped, our Master, himself a Jew, dies a thousand deaths.

Peace is not something to be won by writing essays on racial good will. Peace is not to be achieved by passing resolutions against hatred. Peace must be won right here at home by the incarnation of the gospel of reconciliation within our individual lives and within the life and work of our churches. The symbol of our faith is not a hatchet but a cross.

In the fifth place, our American churches can work for peace by re-establishing fellowship with the Christians of other lands as quickly as possible after the war. To an unprecedented degree the world-wide fellowship of Christians has survived the ravages of military conflict. Never before, in time of war, have Christians made such an effort to preserve intact the ties of spiritual comradeship. In England, ever since the outbreak of the war, the British churches have sponsored Christian fellowship groups with Scandinavian, Czech, Dutch, French, German, and Danish refugees. German pastors driven from the Reich by the Nazi fury have preached in British pulpits. Religious broadcasts originating in London and beamed toward Germany have transmitted to the Christians of that country the gospel of a deathless comradeship in Christ. During more than four years of saber rattling, the World Council of Churches has maintained its contacts with the European churches. German churchmen have commuted back and forth from the German Reich to neutral Switzerland to confer and pray with their Christian colleagues, many of whom were nationals of countries with which Hitler was at war. A considerable number of British churchmen have flown westward across the Atlantic to meet and counsel with American religious leaders. And a considerable number of American churchmen have flown eastward across the Atlantic to meet and counsel with British and European church leaders. A British bishop flew to Stockholm to consider postwar problems with Scandinavian Christians. A bishop of China, the head of the National Christian Council of that country, is in the United States at this very moment. Some months ago churchmen from New Zealand and Australia journeyed to the United States to attend the Princeton Round Table on World Order. American churchmen have flown to Iceland, Greenland, Italy, North Africa, India, and China, always for the purpose of confessing their faith in a Christ whose church transcends the divisions occasioned by war.

Still other American Christians have traveled by sea and by air to South America, to Hawaii and to Alaska, always in the role of good ambassadors of Jesus Christ. At the Princeton round table, in addition to the delegates from New Zealand and Australia, there were present Christians from China, Poland, England, Canada, Germany, Japan, Czechoslovakia, China, Norway, the Netherlands, and Switzerland.

From Princeton there was addressed "A Message to the Many Christians in War-Torn Lands." This message expressed the hope that the Lord God would strengthen the faith of these Christians, and our faith, so that they and we might the better serve God's holy purpose. It is a thrilling story of high adventure and one that will be written large in the history of these stirring times.

In looking to the future, the Princeton message anticipated the sending of Christian missions to the lands ravaged by war. "We long to come to you in person," it was said, "and to bring you some material succor and to receive from you the fuller stimulus of your spiritual vigor. We hope and believe that the time for that is not far distant. We know that there must still be much agony of body and soul. But the end is in sight."

And the end *is* in sight. That is, the end of the military conflict is in sight. But with the termination of the war, there will open to the Christians of the world the door of a very great opportunity. It is hoped that a world conference of Christians may be convened soon after the cessation of hostilities. But more than the convening of a single conference is called for if Christians are to do what then will be required to be done. Plans should be perfected now for the sending of good-will deputations to and from America as quickly as travel facilities become available. I am not thinking of deputations to promote the missionary enterprise, as such, although I can think of nothing that would more effectively accomplish

233

this end. I am thinking of good-will deputations to
and from America that will voice the prayerful concern of Christendom that national prides and prejudices and national bigotries and national power
politics may at long last be brought under the domination of our Lord and Savior Jesus Christ. Let us, on
our part, send a deputation to China to tell the long-
suffering people of that country that we desire for
them the honor and recognition due them as a people
destined to play a major part in the world of tomorrow. And while in China, we might say to the Chinese
people what the Cairo communiqué did not say, that
we desire to see an end, not only of Japanese imperialism in East Asia, but of all imperialism, British
and American included. Let us send a deputation
to Japan to tell the people of that country that the
wounds engendered by war can be healed by Him who
is the Great Physician. And while in Japan, we might
say to the Japanese people what the Cairo communiqué did not say, that we desire for them an opportunity to earn a decent living and to qualify for membership in the family of nations. Let us send a deputation to Africa to make clear the fact that the
churches of America desire for the people of that vast
continent an era of economic, political, and spiritual
enlightenment. Let us send a deputation to Latin
America to' assure the peoples and governments of
these twenty-one republics that Christians in the
United States see in the Good Neighbor policy a means
by which there may be established upon this continent
an era of economic, political, and spiritual reciprocity.

Let us send a deputation to the occupied countries of Europe to tell their religious leaders that the entire Christian world is indebted to them for their brave stand against Nazi tyranny and for their refusal to render unto Caesar the things that belong to God. Let us send a deputation to Germany to re-establish Christian fellowship with the churches of that country, many of whose leaders have been and are now in concentration camps. Let us send a deputation to Russia to establish fraternal relations with the Orthodox churches of that country and to bear testimony to the leaders of the Soviet Government that we in the United states desire to see the suspicion and ill will hitherto prevailing between the two countries forever laid at rest.

And let us make known our readiness, in deep humility of spirit, to receive in our country Christian deputations from all these and other countries. Out of the experience which has been theirs, they will bring to us and to our churches the visible evidences of a Christian discipleship that has prevailed against the military might of nations and empires bent upon the enslavement of religion.

When this war is over, the whole earth will be one vast parish for the exercising of such Christian virtues as charity and reconciliation. Whatever may be the nature of the settlements agreed to now or at the end of the war, there will still remain the task of bringing together in the bonds of unity men of good will of all nations and races. This is pre-eminently the task of the Christian churches. No settlement, no treaty of peace, will be adequate to bridge the chasms by which peoples have been divided during this period of war and bloodletting. This pilgrimage of Christian believers of which I speak will go far toward laying that spiritual foundation upon which it is hoped the new world order may be established. I recommend, therefore, that the responsible heads of our various communions and interdenominational bodies organize at once a planning commission to prepare the way for the launching of this international visitation that may well prove to be the twentieth century counterpart of that first century adventure of Christian fellowship through which the then known world was made to feel the power of the resurrected Lord.

In the sixth place, the churches of America can work for peace by energizing with a spiritual purpose the postwar planning of human intelligence. By rededicating our churches to the task of evangelism, which is the primary duty laid upon us by our Lord, we shall be making a contribution to world order, the effects of which may not be immediately discernible, but which will in the long run provide the only foundation upon which a just and durable peace can be established. It is for the churches to say that the ills with which the world is beset cannot wholly be cured by political or economic readjustments. Today's war is only in part the evil contriving of Adolf Hitler and the Japanese war lords. What we are witnessing today is the Armageddon of a proud and arrogant secularism. Our education, our science, our statecraft, and in some respects our culture are contaminated with the virus of a self-seeking materialism. The power worshiped by the modern world is the power of rocket guns and bombing planes, of political prestige, of territorial possessions, of markets and material treasure. The voice of the churches, therefore, must be a voice crying in the wilderness. And this voice must be the voice of repentance. Let the churches of the world say to their respective governments: "Repent! Repent of your slavish obedience to the siren call of sovereign power. Repent of your adoration of the might of tanks and howitzers and armies and navies. Repent of your long-delayed concession of freedom for subject peoples. Repent of your policies of encirclement, of your drawing of boundary lines to meet the requirements of power politics, of your coalitions and your military alliances."

Where, save in the religion of Jesus Christ, can this confused and misdirected generation discover the power sufficient to transcend the cleavages by which the secular world is so tragically divided against itself? The differences in political ideology and economic theory and cultural patterns can never be synthesized by a military victory of the United Nations. The churches can make their most distinctive and effective contribution to the winning of the peace by making new men and new women and by generating and making available to the world the spiritual power which alone can achieve a synthesis of conflicting loyalties for the common good.

Political and economic interpretations of history, when stripped of their academic verbiage, reveal a philosophy of life and a conception of the universe which are pagan to the core. There is not nor can there be any fixed purpose to which humans may repair if history and the march of events are to be interpreted solely in terms of political and economic directives. When, just prior to the outbreak of the war, Hitler entered into a nonaggression pact with Stalin, the Communists in England and in the United States launched an assault of abuse and of sabotage against the nations of the West. When this pact of nonaggression was broken by Hitler and the *Wehrmacht* goose-stepped its way into Russia, the Communists reversed their tactics and launched their assault of abuse and sabotage against Hitler and the Axis nations. This is an illustration of the illogical ends to which humans are inexorably driven when they are motivated by materialistic conceptions of history. Over against these variables of the secular world we of the churches must point to Him who is the guiding star both for our little day and for the centuries.

Let the churches therefore possess for themselves and propagate to the ends of the earth a faith that will reflect the rhythm of the divine purpose for the world and for the children of men. Let us rise above the spirit of defeatism which in certain instances has decimated even the ranks of Christian believers and lay hold upon the power possessed in such great abundance by the early Christians who turned the Roman Empire upside down. And they did this, not

238

by adopting resolutions nor by lowering their banners to the level of the secular community; they did this by making Christians out of pagans and by standing before princes and potentates and saying with a reckless but a God-inspired abandon, "Thus saith the Lord."

Let the churches of America arise. Let them sing for peace for theirs is a song augmented by the choirs of heaven. Let them pray for peace, for theirs is a prayer that has been wafted heavenward by the saints and seers of ages past. Let them work for peace, for theirs is a labor to which they have been summoned by Him who is the world's peace. Those of you who are preachers, will you not in your sermons lift yourselves above the level of newspaper headlines and proclaim the truth that nations are to be judged by the God of history? Will you not forego thoughts of ecclesiastical preferment and think only of standing before your people as the apostles of a deathless Christ who counted it an honor to die upon a cross that in dying he might draw the world unto himself! Will you not divest yourselves of the doubts with which you are now possessed and believe that the might of principalities and powers as evidenced by belching guns and bombing planes is not to be compared with the might embodied in the Sword of the Spirit? Will you not believe, as St. Augustine believed, that amidst the wreckage and the desolation of a dying civilization, there may be seen the City of God? And you who are laymen, will you not remember that you walk in the footsteps of those first century Christians who with bleeding feet traveled over paths of pain and of persecution that they might introduce Jesus Christ to a proud and boastful and arrogant society? Will you not remember that you are priests of God, and prophets of God, and that to you no less than to your ministers, there has been delegated the responsibility of manifesting in your lives a loyalty to God which supersedes all lesser loyalties? If you, who are laymen, will give to your church a devotion which reaches beyond your devotion to service clubs and lodges and political organizations, we shall have a church in America that will be a power for peace and for righteousness. The time has come for you laymen to vote your religion and not your politics, to recognize in Jesus Christ an authority which is more binding upon you than are the norms of conduct fixed by the secular community. If you who are preachers and laymen will have the vision and the daring to establish in your churches an altar to which all may come regardless of color or social status, we shall have a Christian community possessed of the dynamic and revolutionary power required to establish upon the earth a warless world.

THE CHURCH AND THE NEW WORLD MIND

Rufus M. Jones*

THERE is no question that this is one of those moments in history which is a crisis epoch in the life of the world, and Christianity is, without doubt, at the center of the crisis. Everything which concerns the issues of human life on this earth is being tried and tested by what the Book of Acts calls "Euroclydon," which is sweeping over its entire surface, and nothing that emerges after the storm has passed will ever be the same again that it was before Euroclydon came down upon it.

Only a major prophet of the highest order could predict at this time what is to happen in any sphere of world events for the next generation. And there is no such prophet. The secret is kept. There is nobody who knows. No sociable angel has up till now whispered the future course of events in any of our ears. Who could have dreamed when Erasmus edited his Greek New Testament, or when Luther nailed his Ninety-five Theses on the church door at Wittenberg, what these things would do for the spirit of man during the next four hundred years? Of course, nobody, least of all Erasmus or Luther themselves, could foresee the future. We are living, as they were, in a catastrophic epoch when all values are undergoing revaluation, and everything that can be shaken will be

---

*This lecture was prepared by Dr. Jones for delivery at the conference, but he was unable to attend because of illness.

removed and only *those things which cannot be shaken will remain as they were.* The most I can do on this occasion, therefore, will be, not to predict what is going to happen, but to feel after those aspects of life and religion which are eternally grounded and to indicate, with considerable modesty, what *ought to happen,* at least in the sphere of the Christian church.

I shall be compelled to say here at the beginning, for the honor of truth, that a disturbing feature of the crisis is the fact that so much of present-day Christianity in many parts of the world is enfeebled and ineffective, static and weak in heat and light and power, though there are strong churches and some splendid leaders. The church saved civilization when the Roman Empire fell and very largely shaped the lives on which the new world order was rebuilt. This creative work was due in large measure to the fact that men of tremendous faith, like St. Augustine, St. Jerome, Athanasius, and St. Gregory the Great, especially St. Augustine, were prophet-statesmen and saw in forecast the eternal principles which should undergird the new order, and they drafted the blueprint of the roads and bridges over which the builders of the new epochs were to travel. St. Jerome gave the succeeding generations the Latin Bible; Athanasius, of an earlier date, gave the church its orthodox theological creed; and St. Augustine and St. Gregory the Great struck out the architectural plan for an imperial church of the ages which awed the pagans who overran the world, convinced and convicted them, disciplined their minds, ruled their wills, and formed out

242

of these new and conquering races a better stock of peoples than those that formed the old empire; and they, in turn, created a new world order of a novel type.

But their drafts and their charts and their creeds and their statesmanship will not serve for our new time. We must do our building and make our own highways for life and thought to travel over, though we can at least learn from them that nothing short of that same tremendous faith which animated those former leaders, and nothing less than their type of prophetic statesmanship, adapted to the new time, will serve for this Euroclydon crisis. There is no great future for any people whose faith has burned out or congealed. History records the ominous fact that national degeneration takes place where faith and vision fail or wane as surely as it does when economic assets shrink or when there is a dearth of sound money currency. It is at least as important in this crisis of ours to foster a great vital faith as it is to conserve rubber or steel or gasoline or coal or sugar.

If, therefore, we are to deal wisely with the mission of the church in connection with the new world order, our first concern must be with the revitalization of Christianity and with the discovery of adequate spiritual resources for the new epoch. The age-long civilization of the world which has for generations comfortably housed us is tottering. The pyramid has been balanced on its apex and not established on a broad base. The hour has struck to look to the bases of life and civilization and culture and religion. Despite

the appalling sacrifices, we shall not get the new world
of our hopes, even after the victory in the field is won,
unless we lay the foundations for our new order on
the solid ground of a great faith and vision—faith in
God, faith in Christ, faith in the living Spirit, operating here and now in our world, and faith in man and
his immortal destiny.

We have learned how to hitch our wagons to a star,
as Emerson advised us a hundred years ago to do.
We tap the forces of the universe for our power and
our speed. We turn a button and start our car. We
turn a button and light our house from the inexhaust-
ible storehouse of the universe. We set the furnace
going with another button, and with still another one
we put the refrigerator into operation. We can beat
the antelope on the ground and outfly the eagle in the
air. But none of these achievements give us the true
stature of a person made in the divine image, nor do
they furnish the assurance that this material type of
civilization has any guarantee of future stable per-
manence.

Let us see clearly what the task is that confronts
the church, what Christianity has to face in this new
time. There has come in my life span the greatest
intellectual revolution that has occurred in the entire
history of the race. It began, of course, before I was
born, but the full significance of it has burst in on our
minds in my life period. The sky is no longer thought
of as a series of celestial crystalline domes, with lu-
minous mansions up there for immortal souls, and

with God at the empyrean of this heavenly world. No, it is just space up there with suns and moons and stars and galaxies, and beyond these more suns and moons and stars and galaxies. We are staggered with the distances and with the innumerable world systems, but it is all homeless as a region for souls.

Instead of a fixed date when the heavens and the earth, the firmament and the waters under the firmament, were created by divine fiat, time has been stretched out just as space has been, and we have another astronomical series of figures for the time process of the geological formation of the world and for the stages of unfolding life.

The prevailing tendency of the laboratory method has been to explain each advancing stage in the natural process by antecedent causes and to end, as was bound to happen with that method, with a materialistic and mechanistic universe, or at least with no clew to any reality beyond the cosmic stuff itself. Psychology has tended to interpret mind processes in terms of brain processes and glands, and there has been no adequate interpretation to our college youth of the unique spirit in man and its transcendent possibilities. Our higher education has been seriously weak in its interpretation of sound ethical conceptions and no less weak in what should be a constructive philosophical theory of the universe and of mind in man. We are bound to be in a confused welter in thinking about major issues of life, if the basic conceptions of metaphysics and moral action are to be

245

mainly settled in "bull sessions," or by professors
who themselves are adrift on these major issues of
life.

Meantime the Holy Scriptures of the Old and New
Testaments, which for centuries have stood unshaken
as a revelation of God and as a chart of human life,
have undergone the most searching criticism that any
documents in the world have ever received. There
have, of course, been many persons in large areas of
the country who have closed their minds to these revolutionary invasions of thought. They have held
stoutly to their inherited stock of religious ideas and
closed their minds to the new critical interpretations.
What was good enough for Mother has been good
enough for them. But this closed-mind method has
not protected their educated children from the invasion of the floating thistledown seeds of revolutionary
thought, everywhere abroad, nor have *they* succeeded
in dealing successfully with the large element of fact
and truth in the new teachings of the time. They have,
furthermore, been powerless to effect a fresh and
creative reinterpretation of Christian faith which
could meet the deepest issues of modern life and
thought and could awaken the world with a trans-
forming conviction of authentic tidings.

They know that something is radically wrong with
the prevailing interpretation of life and of the universe and of the sacred literature which fed the souls
of our fathers, but they can meet it only with a protest of denial, and they are unable to penetrate their

epoch with a message of life that carries overwhelming conviction to the educated mind.

Meantime the totalitarian experiments of our time have been giving us appalling illustrations of the spiritual nakedness in which the soul of man is left when these materialistic conceptions of the universe and of life are pushed to their logical results and are translated into deed and action on a large scale. Here human life is reduced to a bare biological status. Man becomes, as Shakespeare would say, "a forked radish with a head fantastically carved." The universe is a vast single-story system of cause and effect. It is hard, cruel, and spiritually empty. The survival of the best race takes the place of the immortal destiny of the individual person. And the "best" race is the one that does "survive." The sacred books of pagan ancestors tend to be substituted for the Book of the Hebrew prophets and of the gentle Christ, who let himself be crucified instead of leading a furious attack, a "blitz" assault, on the conquerors of his country.

The significant task of the church, of organized Christianity, as I see it, is to give to our time and to our complex age, confused with its materialistic trends, a fresh, creative and thought-convicting interpretation of the universe, of history, of life, of self-conscious spirit in man, of immortal destiny, of divine revelation, of the Christ of Galilee and Bethany, and of the eternal Christ as a continuing Presence with us here and now in our joys and sorrows, and finally of the possibility of direct and immediate experience

247

of the reality of God, because we are so made that "spirit with Spirit can meet."

Whatever happens to our world now, we must keep the Christian church at its spiritual mission. And if we are to rebuild the broken world on right lines we Christians must get together and we must work together. I am not concerned for the moment about what is known as "organic union," or "ecumenical" fusion. I hope there will always be denominations, or at least vital cells, that maintain a peculiar emphasis on important aspects of religious faith and life which other branches of the church are apt to forget or overlook. But these denominational fences must never be so "sheep-high, bull-strong, and pig-tight" that we cannot all, as followers of Christ, work together cooperatively for fresh forward movements of the Spirit and for the building of a better world for children to be born into. One trouble is that these denominational fences are sometimes like Robinson Crusoe's fence for his goats, so large that the goats inside the fence became as wild as those outside the fence were!

What I am mainly concerned with in this lecture is the spiritual preparation of the Christian church to fit it for constructive leadership not only for America but for the world, and my central point of emphasis is the necessity that the Christian leaders of our time and generation equip the church to become the purveyor of a message, an interpretation of life, as adequate for our epoch as St. Augustine's was for the epoch when the Roman Empire collapsed.

This interpretation must begin, I think, if it is to be effective with the youth of today, with a rediscovery of the unique spiritual range and scope of *personal life in man.* It is here that we must come to grips with the major enemy of Christianity, which is a stark materialism. It is here, in the operation of spirit in man, that the Ariadne clew must be found to guide us from the sheer biological level of human life to the reality of a being that bears within the revealing marks of a higher origin, and that partakes of a two-story structure, an upper and a lower level. There is a Jacob's ladder within this unique inward self of ours that reaches another realm than that of matter, and we must make that fact a central issue of our faith. I am not ashamed of the hairs on my arms or of the caudal coccyx below, which point to an animal ancestry in my physical structure, so long as I have the inward evidence that I carry at the center of my being an emergent contribution of spirit from that *deeper world* within the world we see, "whereof this world is but the bounding shore." There is something of God revealed in this inmost capacity of ours —something that is spirit and not matter, something that bears the image of an Eternal Creator.

We look out at every moment of our self-conscious lives upon each new fact of knowledge from a uniquely unified comprehensive self which binds the new fact into an enduring self which not only knows the fact, but also knows itself as knowing it. If that capacity were lost, we should at once lose our personal identity.

This emergent self of ours, all the time, in every experience, is beyond, that is, transcends, what is before it as a given fact. We carry a beyond within us. To be conscious of a limit is to be already beyond it. There is an imaginative dominion in us which out-reaches every limit at which we arrive. Like the Magi we are star-led. The capacity for ideal vision is built into our structure. It is one of our most significant traits. All our discoveries, all our advances, are due to the soul's invincible surmise, which in the sphere of religion we call faith, or insight, or vision. It has given us our prophets, our saints, our mystics, as well as all our discoverers and our inventors.

> This life were brutish did we not sometimes
> Have intimations clear of wider scope,
> Hints of occasion infinite, to keep
> The soul alert with noble discontent
> And onward yearnings of unstilled desire.[1]

We are made that way and we shall never lose that trait of following the star so long as we are persons.

All our values of life attach to this unique spiritual self of ours. There is no joy in beauty until there is an appreciative self of this higher order, and then the whole universe, even "in the mud and scum of things," is crammed with beauty. Here we rise entirely above matter and mechanism and cause and effect, and are already in a realm of a higher order. We are, too, in this higher realm whenever we dis-

---

[1] From "The Cathedral," by James Russell Lowell. Used by permission of Houghton Mifflin Co., publishers.

cover *what eternally ought to be,* and dedicate our
lives to the achievement of what is beautifully, that is,
essentially, good.   There is in us, too, a capacity to
love, not for the sake of returns, not from the spur
of sex, but because soul discovers soul and is enamored
with a pure passion of unselfish, self-giving love.

Love took up the harp of Life, and smote on all the
    chords with might;
Smote the chord of Self, that, trembling, pass'd in
    music out of sight.[2]

There is no higher evidence of this uniqueness than
our capacity for *truth.*   We are essentially truth seek-
ers.   The science of the ages, forever pursuing, forever correcting, holding firmly to what resists all at-
tempts to doubt it, is evidence enough that a type of
mind is operating above the welter of events and that
it is a mind which, within a narrow sphere, has apo-
dictic, that is, absolute, certainty.   There are some
realities for mind that *must be so.*   Nothing in this
world of ours is more revealing of our junction with
a Beyond than are these ideal values of beauty, truth,
goodness, and unselfish love.

And throughout the entire history of the race, there
has been a succession of persons, with special gifts
of grace, who have had mutual and reciprocal corre-
spondence with an overworld of Spirit that was as
real and certain to them as their own central existence.   They have known God, as George Fox put it,

---

[2]From ''Locksley Hall,'' by Alfred Tennyson.   Used by permission of the Macmillan Co., publishers.

"experimentally." They have discovered and practiced His presence, with joy and radiance. And for
the most part, these open-windowed souls have lived
under a spell of immortal life. They have felt links
with eternity. They have found themselves living in
a two-story universe with a Home in it for all we love,
and a Garden greater than Eden, where transplanted
human worth will bloom to profit otherwhere. What
I want to see is a church that interprets human life
convincingly on these creative lines, and then it can
inspire and form the new world mind.

But, of course, this mission of interpretation which
I have sketched for the church is not an adequate one
—if it stopped here it would be incomplete. The
church must once more put the Bible in its exalted
place as the supreme spiritual literature of the ages.
These books of revelation must once more be built
into the mental fiber of our youth to go no more out.
The Bible has come through the critical researches of
a hundred years as a more vital revelation than ever
before. It must be taken as settled that there is a
human element in it, and that it is marked by the
epochs and stages through which the human race has
passed; but *that* ought always to have been recognized. It could hardly speak to our condition today
if it were not so. No one could ever mistake Samson
for St. John. The Bible has become, or at least can
become, for the modern man a *live* book. The prophets stand forth now in full stature among the supreme
geniuses of the race. The Book of Job is one of the
greatest epics of human life the world possesses. The

Psalms are unique and speak appealingly to every age of life. The Gospels are the most precious spiritual documents in existence. St. Paul is now seen to be one of the most discerning interpreters of life that has ever been on the planet, the greatest missionary that ever lived, and the creative builder of the church which we have inherited. The Bible is the sifted literature of the Spirit and par excellence the revelation of God to men through the ages, the written chart of the way of life. Bibliolatry is always a mistake, it is always unintelligent. But unless we are to put civilization and culture in peril, the church must put the Bible back into its right place as a foundation of true spiritual training and as an essential mental stock of children's education for life.

The church must constantly go back to the headwaters of its faith and keep vivid in its thought and ministry the life, the teaching, the ministry, the mission, the self-giving sacrifice, and the triumphant survival of the great Galilean Founder of our Christianity. In Him we find, not a new creed, not a new ritual, not a new theology, not a new authoritative ecclesiastical foundation, but a new type of Person, who revealed the heart and character of God, and at the same time exhibited the divine possibilities of man as a child of God and as a member of the Kingdom of God.

The church of the present and the future cannot lead the world on its way and cannot take the lead in the formation of the new world mind unless Christ is vitally and vividly at the creative center of its life

253

and leadership. And he must be seen not only as the unique Person who lives in the pages of the Four Gospels, and who walked the hills of Galilee; he must be felt and known as the eternal *living* Christ, forever being born anew in the lives of his loving followers. No dead fact stranded on the shore of the oblivious years—

> But warm, sweet, tender, even yet
> A present help is He;
> And faith has still its Olivet,
> And love its Galilee.
>
> The healing of His seamless dress
> Is by our beds of pain;
> We touch Him in life's throng and press,
> And we are whole again.

Something like this, I predict, must be the message and the mission of the church of the future, if it is to have genuine leadership in rebuilding the broken world, and if it is to be a creative factor in shaping the new world mind.

But it is of no avail to talk of the church in general, the church in the abstract, unless the concrete particular local church which the people attend can become a center of light and leading, of inspiration and guidance, for its specific community.

The vital end which really concerns us in this conference is, in the final issue, how to make the actual church that the people attend a living cell of spiritual power for its community. There is in almost every college and university a group, larger or smaller, of awakened youth, eager for reality, swept with a yearning for enlarged life and for spiritual adventure. Too often, when they return home to their own community, they do not find a church that speaks to their condition. They drift away and are lost to the forces of organized Christianity. It is estimated that there are 1,500,000 Protestant Christians in the city of New York who are not attached to any church in that city. Conditions no doubt similar to that exist in the other large cities of America. Some way must be found to draw these "prepared people" into the vital fellowship of the church. There must be more vitality, more reality, more convincing power, more joy and radiance in the church life and service of the community. In every group that assembles, there are persons perplexed by mysteries of pain and agony, of life and death, and of the terrible problems of sin and evil. Such persons want a fresh prophetic interpretation of life that enables them to stand the universe triumphantly and become equipped and girded to go out with kindled vision to have a part in remaking the world on better lines.

It is one of the most urgent of all our religious tasks to vitalize the rural church and make it minister adequately to its surrounding community life. The world rests on the shoulders of the people who make up these local communities. Six presidents of the United States were born in log cabins; five others were the sons of farmers; three were sons of artisans; and three were children of country parsons. It is persons like these tillers of the land who "maintain the fabrics of the world." We have no more Western frontiers to conquer, and now we must reconquer the rural areas of the country and rear once more in them the vital stock as the foundation material for a great moral and spiritual nation. And that means that the rural church must be the vital cell of the community— a spiritual breeding center for men and women of creative influence for our national life.

Our American missionaries who have created the universities and colleges in the Near East and the twelve Christian universities in China have done very much toward producing the new mental and spiritual atmosphere of these regions of the globe and the awakening of their youth. If our American Christianity can now awake and arise to its divine possibilities and find its new skyline, it may become the quickening force that will help to penetrate the lands both in the East and in the West, now in desolation, with fresh spiritual insight and power; and there may come to birth a new world mind that will reshape the destiny of man in ways of enduring and constructive peace.

I may very well close this address with a wise sentence from my beloved William James: "There is but one unconditional commandment, which is that we should seek incessantly, with fear and trembling, so to vote and to act as to bring about the very largest total universe of good which we can see."[3]

---

[3]From *The Will to Believe*, p. 209. Used by permission of Longmans, Green & Co., publishers.